THE KOREAN KITCHEN
Recipes from the Land of the Morning Calm

---

by
COPELAND MARKS
with
MANJO KIM

CHRONICLE BOOKS
SAN FRANCISCO

Library of Congress Cataloging-in-Publication Data

Marks, Copeland.
    The Korean Kitchen: Classic recipes from the Land of the Morning Calm/
by Copeland Marks.
        p.   cm.
    Includes bibliographical references and index.
    ISBN 0-8118-0321- X
    1. Cookery, Korean.   I. Title.
    TX724.5.K65M37   1993
    641.59519—dc20   92-38968
                                                                                  CIP

Printed in The United States of America.

Distributed in Canada by Raincoast Books, 112 East Third Ave.,
Vancouver, B.C. V5T 1C8

10 9 8 7 6 5 4 3 2 1

Chronicle Books
275 Fifth Street
San Francisco, CA 94103

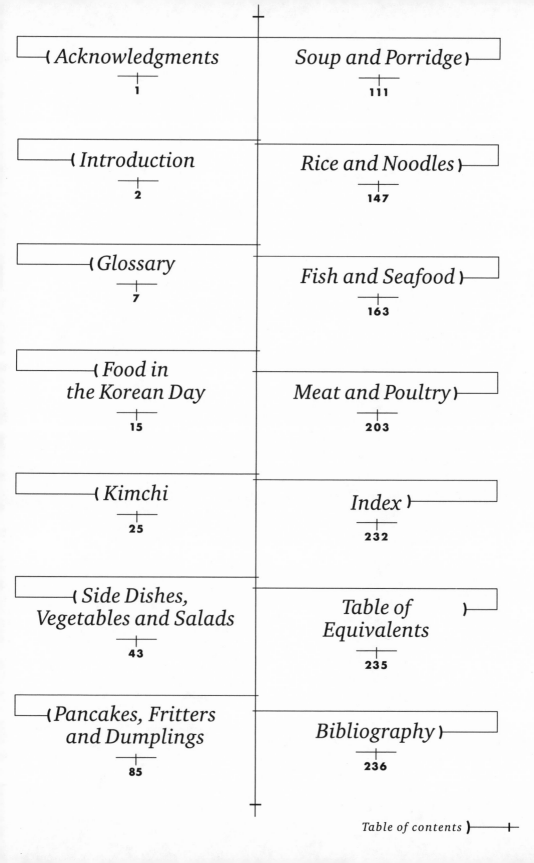

Table of contents

Acknowledgments

Uncovering the fascinating mysteries of Korean cooking was not accomplished with a magic wand. The Korea National Tourism Corporation offered their good offices and assistance, especially in Korea. Korean Airlines transported me in more ways than one to and from Korea.

Of the many women who were responsible for revealing the history, technique, and philosophy of Korean cooking, Bokkyu Song, He Suk Im (Holly) and Amy Hai Kyung Lee devoted time, effort and their considerable knowledge to my search. Lou Ann Smith provided the original catalyst for my project.

My very special admiration is reserved for Dr. (Mrs.) Manjo Kim whose encyclopedic knowledge of all facets of the Korean cuisine was indispensable. Mr. Won Kyung Cho added to my cultural knowledge and shared many recipes.

To others in the cities of Korea who provided many weeks of the pleasures of dining, cooking and learning, I offer my enthusiastic thanks.

Introduction

When researching this book, I found to my surprise that Korea contains the best-kept culinary secret in Asia. It has the most relevant cuisine for our time, with a complete commitment to a healthy diet—greens, grains, a smaller amount of meat, low cholesterol, low fat, but all well seasoned—in fact, all the magic formulae that we believe guarantee long life. The Korean cuisine with its savory, idiosyncratic flavors and the abundant resources from its fields and the sea, has it all.

In the first place, Korea is completely surrounded by water—from the Yalu River in the mountainous North to the East China Sea at its southern tip; from the Sea of Japan on the East to the Yellow Sea on the West (Koreans refer to them as the South, East and West Seas). They are the lifeblood (and food source) of the nation. Koreans from the central core of the country, as well as those from the coastal sections, look seaward for their culinary inspiration as well as for every other aspect of their daily lives.

Koreans are descended from a Mongolian race who came south from Mongolia and Manchuria and developed into a distinct nationality of great individuality—honed by the vicissitudes of life in a rugged country and beset by innumerable Japanese invasions. A feisty, provincial people, bursting with energy and goodwill, tough and intelligent, they have maintained their identity, their own language and customs, with admirable firmness and a strong belief in their own culture and religion.

The development of Korea over the centuries is the story of ancient dynasties in a hereditary, aristocratic ruling structure. In a system of monarchy, a few sovereigns reigned over the village slaves and peasants who made up the predominant population.

It was the dynastic organization and the historical experience of their authority that led the country onward to its modern development. The Koguyro dynasty (37 B.C. to 668 A.D.) probably gave Korea its name. The Silla dynasty (57 B.C. to 935 A.D.) was famous for its artistic endeavors, from its temples to the tombs where so many artifacts of culture were buried. But rule by the dynasties ended with the Choson or Yi dynasty (1392 to 1910), when Korea became a "protectorate" of Japan.

When dynasties create artistic masterpieces, it is arguably logical that they also create culinary dishes that reflect their royal status. Unfortunately, I have not uncovered anything to prove this, although my intuition tells me that it must be true. There are, however, two categories of food that have survived—that of the peasant and that of the royal palace. This is known to be the case with the Choson (Yi) dynasty.

There is a Korean attitude regarding food that defines their philosophy at the table. The philosophy of a good life is a combination of Confucianism and Buddhism. Wholesomeness is represented by the food served and the treatment and respect accorded to it. Since women are the cooks in Korea, the emotional feeling that the mother possesses is expressed through her use of the natural crops collected from the fields and mountains, such as wild mushrooms, greens, edible roots. If the mother loves her family and guests, the food itself will be collected and prepared with care. The mother will exhibit affection by serving a variety of freshly made dishes as a stable, emotional expression of family life.

Korea is an eating society. City streets are lined with one eating house after another, each serving its regional specialties. A few tables and chairs (to seat about 20), a simple ambience and reasonable prices are common. Order a main dish and you will be served the inevitable kimchi and 4 or 5 side dishes of vegetables, anchovy condiment and cold soup. Most dishes are loaded with garlic or Korea's beloved and indispensable hot red chili powder.

Koreans are night people. During the day they work industriously at their pursuits, as is their custom. After dark, the streets bustle, especially in Seoul and Pusan in the South. The women vendors bring out their bag of tricks—specialties that are popular and easily transported. In Pusan, the Street of Eats is a joy. Beef strips and rice rolls in a tomato and hot chili sauce are sizzling on gas griddles. Side dishes of several types and their soy sauce dips are standing by to be taken on a help-yourself basis. Competitors selling the same foods are neck and neck, sitting on the narrow road closed to vehicular traffic. Very little meat is seen except the roasted, bronze-colored pigs' feet, which look wonderful but are hard as rocks. Street food is cheap, à la carte and in great demand, especially after dark.

Perhaps the most famous Korean food is the one known internationally as *kimchi*, preserved vegetables. There are an estimated 200 varieties of kimchi such as cabbage, cucumber, eggplant, Korean radish, turnip. Filled with vitamins and minerals and distinguished by the hot chili, kimchi has been a staple in the Korean diet since ancient times.

The Korean fascination with the chili is in itself a fascinating story since the chili originated botanically in the Valley of Mexico and Guatemala. The chili, which plays a central part in the high voltage cooking of Korea, has developed a significance of its own in denoting the machismo of how much one can eat without gasping for breath. Oddly, the red color furnished by the chili predominates in Korean food, yet the tomato, which also originated in Central America, did not make the same headway in the Korean lexicon of ingredients and is hardly ever used. The chili is seen everywhere, drying on roofs in major cities or on a bridge crossing a river, on museum grounds in a southwest Korean town. No spot is sacrosanct when drying the chili.

During the seven-year war that began in 1592 between Japan and Korea, Portuguese Catholic priests accompanied Japanese troops to Korea. The Portuguese took along the chili seeds or plants which the Spanish had brought from Central America to Europe. And so the chili entered Korea via Japan and took hold with a vengeance never to be relinquished. Before the arrival of the chili, during the Tang dynasty in China (618 to 906 A.D.), the Chinese version of hot spice was known as *tang chu*, "the suffering plant," hot on the tongue. I believe this may have been a form of pepper similar to the Szechwan peppercorn used to this day in China.

Various treatises on agriculture were produced in the sixteenth century. Koreans have been preoccupied with health and food since the early Choson (Yi) dynasty, from the sixteenth century and onward, with works on horticulture, livestock and cultivation. In the eighteenth century, sweet potatoes were brought from Japan as a famine prevention food and their use spread rapidly so they became a common item in the diet. The white potato was introduced by the Chinese in approximately 1840 and also became part of the common diet.

Stews of fish, clams, crab, tofu (*tubu*), vegetables, mushrooms both fresh and dried are substantial enough so that the absence of large meat servings is not noticed. Pancakes, called *jon*, of almost unlimited and artful combinations, including fish, seafood, meat and vegetables, are favorites for quick meals, picnics and nibbling at any hour.

Although I did see a few disconsolate ducks for sale in very few public markets, it is safe to state that Koreans as a whole do not eat duck. They say that if you eat duck your feet will become webbed like the feet of ducks! So much for the strange beliefs of others.

Rice is the staff of life and Koreans eat it with everything any time of day. This is not the seasoned rice served in Persia or Indonesia but plain, steamed white rice that constitutes a buffer to the intensity of their chili-hot foods.

The Korean table does not groan with huge quantities of food but it does whisper with an assortment of side dishes with each meal. Dips, hot sauces, kimchi, pickled fish or crab and soups adorn a table in small but telling quantity and variety.

Bulgogi is the famous (at least in Asia) Korean barbecue in which very thin strips of beef, fat free (the most popular), chicken, squid or octopus are marinated in seasonings and grilled.

Fruit is plentiful but for the most part eaten as it comes—not cooked or made into pies or puddings. Dried fruit is sometimes used in a stew or to make a drink, but the fresh fruit is usually served raw and whole as a snack or at the end of a meal.

Kwanju is a remarkably traditional city for this technological age, situated in southwestern Korea. It is well known throughout Korea for the establishment of its own style of cooking. For about 3,500 years, its abundant natural resources helped to develop its way of life. Rice and barley at that time became the chief foods. A particular method of preparing side dishes, its use of luxury items in foods, plus the introduction of serving utensils were all influential in the genesis of the cuisine. Metal tablespoons appeared as well as metal chopsticks with long tapered ends.

Cabbage kimchi, various wild greens, the sesame leaf with its faint anise flavor, fish stews, boiled foods, meat roasted with seasonings, added to the assortment of the culture of food.

Dishes incorporated such unconventional mixtures as boiled rice and barley, glutinous rice, rice with sweet potato or millet, rice with black beans, pine nut porridge, octopus porridge, fermented cucumber kimchi, barley soup, clam soup, sesame taffy cakes, steamed eggs, mushrooms, bracken, taro stems, thirty varieties of pickled fish, and pickled fish throat!

Also, seafood soup, beef entrails soup, chicken and rice porridge, beef short ribs, carp and chicken soup, boiled piglet, grilled eel, seasoned bamboo shoots, fried laver, seasoned raw skate, fish eggs, pressed and salted fish roe, pickled crab or oysters—all gave this one city its culinary reputation.

There are now substantial communities of Koreans in many cities around the United States, especially in California and the New York area. Each has its own Little Korea with food shops and supermarkets that cater to the public, selling standard spices and seasonings as well as the exotic ingredients that are used to prepare

Korean dishes. Personally, I do not care to use substitutes if it is possible with judicious shopping to collect everything that is needed.

The American kitchen, always on the alert for new, tasty, healthful ethnic foods, will find in Korean cooking an immediate attraction that can fulfill the new search for good living in an exotic diet.

I suggest that you read this Glossary first for information that will be helpful in reproducing the recipes. All of these ingredients can be found in Korean and other Asian food shops.

CHILI:

FLAKES: Dried hot red chilies are first seeded, then coarsely crushed. They provide heat and are visible, indicating the quantity used.

POWDER (*Gocho Karu*): Chilies are seeded and the dried husk is ground to a fine powder. The powder is used as a coloring agent as well as distributing the heat uniformly in kimchi. The dried seeds are occasionally used in kimchi.

THREADS: Chili threads are dried hot red chilies cut into the thinnest 2- or 3-inch-long threads imaginable. These are decorative in nature and provide a modest sting to the food. Wandering through the public markets in Korean cities, but especially in Pusan, I saw village women selling small mounds of these chili threads for a few pennies. The dried chilies are seeded and cut with scissors into the red hairlike lengths. Only someone with the patience of Job would undertake that kind of daunting work. Now, the threads are cut by machine.

CHINESE CHIVES or KOREAN LEEK (*Allium odoratum*): A common sight in Chinese and Korean markets. The long, green, slender chive leaves are tied up in bunches and sold by the pound. The root bulbs have been neatly trimmed off. Although they resemble scallions in flavor, they do not have a pronounced onion aroma. Used in a number of dishes but conspicuous in kimchi.

CHRYSANTHEMUM LEAVES (*Chrysanthemum coronarium*): Most chrysanthemum leaves are edible but not all are palatable. This botanical variety is the recommended one. The leaves of this ornamental plant have no bitterness and are used raw in salads, stir-fry dishes and soup. The Koreans refer to the edible leaves as *sookgat*. A botanical garden catalogue refers to the leaves as "chop suey greens."

CORVINA (*Micropogon undulatus*): Known as *chogi* in Korea. A popular fish, yellow in color and recommended for certain fish preparations.

DENJANG PASTE: A fermented soybean paste and flavor enhancer. One of the most important standard seasonings in the Korean firmament. It can be and is prepared at home in the large, black ceramic pots so conspicuous on rooftops in the cities and in farmhouse areas. The commercial denjang sold in Korean markets is excellent and one only has to select a brand that is appealing.

Denjang matures like old wine and can be kept for a very long time, ten to thirty years. Conservative families renew the paste each year so the flavor is ever-changing. The soybeans differ in flavor, so does water, the seasonings and therefore the fermented denjang itself. Families remember the taste of the paste in previous years, the differences in intensity and the pleasure of dining with a perfectly fermented batch.

Koji is an academic term for the microbiological starter used to prepare the denjang. The very soft, cooked soybeans are crushed and mixed with the starter. The beans must be cooled after cooking. If the temperature is 150°F. or above it will kill the useful microbes that are necessary to ferment the beans.

DRIED ANCHOVY: Dried anchovies are an important adjunct to the Korean kitchen. All sizes are used in one form or another. I first encountered anchovy water in a small eating house near a bus station in Kyongju. The cooks, waiters and the owner were women, and the 6-year-old son of the manager was removing the dishes from the tables. Here is how it is made: The large dried anchovies, about 3 inches long, are soaked in water to cover in a large ceramic pot all day. The liquid is strained and the anchovies are discarded. It is this strained liquid that is used in preparing soups and stews.

Small dried anchovies about 1 inch in length are used to prepare the tasty side dish, Myulchi Boekum, with its sweet and hot flavor. The same small anchovies are processed to a smooth powder and give a soup dish such as Tubu Kook a seafood flavor.

EGGPLANT, ASIAN (*Solanum melongena*): These are the long, slender eggplants found all over Asia and particularly in Korea where their color is an intense purple. They have very few seeds, unlike the oval supermarket variety found in the United States, and do not require peeling.

FERN, FIDDLEHEAD (*Pteridium aquilinum*): Edible fern or bracken can be purchased throughout the year in Korean or Japanese food stores packed in plastic bags. The fern is about 7 inches long with the rounded violinlike head curled in a tight circle. I have seen the fern heads dried in Korea and the very fresh fronds for sale in New York's open-air vegetable markets in the early summer.

FISH SAUCE: Koreans prepare their own fish sauce by crushing salted, preserved, very small anchovies or shrimps into a smooth paste which is then diluted with water. It is added to soup and other dishes to taste since the sauce is salty with the power of the sea. Bottled fish sauce imported from Thailand and known as Nam Plah is a handy substitute. The sauce is used in several countries in Southeast

Asia. Indonesians use Trassi, a preserved fish paste that produces the same taste effect as a liquid sauce.

GOCHU JANG, Hot Fermented Chili Paste: *Gochu* means chili, and *jang*, a salt-based flavoring sauce. This is the principal standard seasoning in Korean cooking. For centuries it was prepared at home and stored in the ubiquitous black pottery pots so conspicuous on the rooftops or in the gardens in Korea.

On March 3 of each year, an auspicious date, the householder prepares the *gochu jang* that is to be used all year. It consists of sweet (glutinous) rice cooked into a melted mélange. Into this are mixed a fermented soybean cake, hot red chili, salt and malt syrup prepared from barley and water. The mixture is allowed to ferment in a jar for a minimum of 3 months.

As the summer approaches, especially in early May when the sun appears more frequently, the cover of the storage jar is removed early in the day so that the sun can strike and warm the contents to accelerate fermentation. At night the cover is replaced.

The *gochu jang* is ultimately reduced to a smooth jamlike consistency with a many-dimensioned flavor. The paramount seasoning is provided by the hot chili and modified somewhat by the salt and lightly sweet malt syrup. The sweet rice gives it the conserve consistency. *Gochu jang* provides a sting and a rich red color to the food. Korean cooking without this indispensable condiment is unthinkable.

KOREAN DATES or **JUJUBES** (*Ziziphus jujuba*): These plump, red-skinned, firm-fleshed fruits grow on forty-foot-high trees and sometimes on large bushes, from southeast Europe to China and Korea. Used as dried, preserved, stewed fruit and candy. Grow where it is hot and dry.

MEENARI, Korean Watercress (*Oenanthe stolonifera*): This is not the common supermarket watercress found in the United States. Although it is a similar green leafy plant, the taste is different, perhaps more intense. The *meenari* grows in ditches, ponds, rice fields and wet places in the lowlands.

MUKHULI, Rice Wine: This is a farmhouse rice wine—a cloudy, slightly milky liquid with a sweet edge, extremely tasty with a moderate alcoholic content depending, of course, upon the quantity you imbibe. I always made a point during my travels in Korea to look for a working-class pub where I could find Mukhuli and Pa Jon, the scallion pancake, served together as a snack. This snack is considered an institution by the aficionados of the wine. At one time, Mukhuli was made all over Korea by farmers and it may still be to some degree. Commercial Mukhuli is also available and to my taste is quite attractive and acceptable.

To prepare Mukhuli one needs a starter to produce the fermentation process. Whole-wheat berries are coarsely crushed and mixed with water to form a rough firm dough. The dough is wrapped in a porous kitchen towel or cheesecloth and left in a warm spot for 3 days, which allows a white mold to form. These brewery-type microbes are what produces the fermentation. The starter, which has become hard due to the evaporation of the moisture at warm temperature, is then crushed to almost powder form.

Sticky or glutinous rice (farmer's choice) is steamed over hot water until soft but not soggy. Starter, rice and water are mixed together and allowed to ferment in a warm spot (80°F.) for 3 days. The rice kernels will float to the top of the bubbling liquid, indicating that the rice wine is ready. The entire mixture is strained, the rice and any solids are discarded, and the wine must then be refrigerated to stop the fermentation process.

A secondary dilution of the wine may take place simply by adding water to the strained fermented rice, mixing it together and straining it once again. The lighter diluted Mukhuli is preferred by some. Mukhuli is served with pickled fish, cooked pork, pancakes of any type as a snack or aperitif.

MUNG BEANS (*Phaseolus aureus*): Most of the bean sprouts available in the United States and Korea are produced by sprouting mung beans in the dark under quite moist conditions. Mung beans are tiny, green round seeds also used in Korea to prepare a paste used in a type of pancake, the Bindaedoek. The beans are soaked in water for 4 hours, which loosens the green outer coating. The skinless yellow beans are then ground into a paste and incorporated into a pancake. It is also possible to purchase the skinless yellow beans in Korean groceries, a recommended convenience.

PERILLA (*P. frutescens*): The beefsteak plant, more commonly known in Korea as wild sesame, is related to the cultivated sesame. The valentine-shaped leaves are sold in thick bundles in the markets. The pungent-flavored fresh leaves are used as a garnish on rice as well as included in soups and stews. It is an annual herb of the mint family grown in Southeast Asia. Plants are about 3 feet high with the edible green leaves. The seeds are used for oil in Korean cooking and occasionally the seeds are ground to a powder and incorporated into soup, giving it more intensity of flavor.

RADISH (*Raphanus sativus*): Erroneously referred to as a turnip but sometimes called Chinese radish. When grown in Korea, as millions of them are, then it is a Korean radish or *muu*. It is a large vegetable from 3 to 10 inches long, or even longer, football-shaped with a firm white flesh. Prepared in many ways, especially as one of the very popular side dishes, and added to a variety of kimchis. The leaves are edible. It is recommended that the radish be purchased, when possible, with a full length of leaves. It should be pointed out that the Japanese daikon is not the Korean radish.

RICE (*Oryza sativa*): Rice is of Asian origin and is the dominant staple in Asia. The following are the 3 principal types.

MEDIUM GRAIN: This is a small, oval-shaped seed, white and solid looking. Koreans use this type almost exclusively; it is sometimes referred to in common parlance as "sticky rice." In New York I use the Nishiki brand, purchased in Asian groceries. The cooked rice is soft and to me melting. The individual grains still manage to retain their shape and do not congeal into a mass when properly cooked.

GLUTINOUS OR SWEET RICE: This grain has an oval, bleached white look and is somewhat larger than the medium-grain variety. It is used in sweet dishes for the most part but is occasionally combined with the medium grain to vary the texture.

LONG GRAIN: This rice is also known in Korea as Vietnam rice since it was imported from that country. It is not much liked and is used only in an emergency when the medium grain is not available. The slim long grains are preferred in the American kitchen for standard culinary activities, especially when cooking Indian or Middle Eastern dishes.

SEAWEED: The Koreans long ago discovered the use of seaweed in their cooking and are aware of its health-giving properties. Seaweed has a high protein content and is said to be rich in vitamins.

KELP (*Ulva conglobata*): Found in Korean food markets neatly packed in plastic bags. The dried weed, in the form of crumbled pieces of about ½-inch size, expands to smooth green sheets when briefly soaked in water. They have the refreshing aroma of the sea and add texture and color to the soup.

LAVER (*Porphyra umbilicalis*): A popular edible seaweed in Korea. It is dark brown, almost black in color when dried, and sold in very thin sheets about 6 x 8 inches in size. It has a crisp, tasty flavor of the sea when seasoned and toasted.

MIYUK (*Undaria pinnatifida*): An edible brown seaweed, dark colored, purchased dry. It is appreciated by women when added to a rejuvenation soup after the birth of a child (see Miyuk Kook page 116).

SALT: Koreans use the coarse sea salt known in the United States as "kosher" salt. Refined table salt is not used for several reasons: it is expensive and may contain added minerals such as iodine, which alter the flavor of food.

I saw several salt-drying pans along the southwest coast of Korea. The seawater is confined to large areas along the coast and is allowed to evaporate during the hot summer days. This system guarantees a constantly renewable source of coarse salt.

SESAME (*Sesamum indicum*): Sesame seeds and oil are one of the most important seasonings in Korean cooking. The toasted seeds are sprinkled on salad side dishes, incorporated into stews, crushed for additional flavor and added to barbecued meat and fish.

SESAME SALT (*How to Make*): Toasted sesame seeds can be purchased, but they are not toasted enough to develop the complete flavor. Put the seeds in a skillet, preferably a nonstick one, and toast over low heat for 2 or 3 minutes, shaking the pan frequently. This should darken the seeds to a light bronze color. Cool and then use them at all times.

2 tablespoons toasted sesame seeds

1 teaspoon coarse salt

Put the sesame seeds and salt in a mortar and pound them to a rough powder. Store in a jar with a tight cover and use when needed.

SESAME OIL: Sesame oil is a flavor and is not generally used as a frying medium. The oil is pressed from the crushed, well-toasted seeds and has a nutlike aromatic flavor. Added to soups, salads, dips and marinades, the oil defines the flavor of Korean cooking. Sesame oil is high in polyunsaturated fat; considering our preoccupation with cholesterol, it is highly recommended for purposes of health.

BLACK SESAME SEEDS: These are unhulled standard sesame seeds, which have the same properties and flavor as the hulled and toasted type. They are used as a decorative garnish.

SOY SAUCE (*How to Brew It*): Soybeans are cooked slowly in water and salt for 6 to 8 hours. When the beans are soft enough to be crushed between the fingers, they are done.

There are two methods of crushing the soft cooked beans. One is to mash them with a mallet. The second method, country style, is to pour them in a cloth bag, tie it up, then stomp on the bag to crush the beans into a paste; old-fashioned but effective.

The paste is then put into ball-shaped straw containers. The ball is small enough (about 1 measuring cup) so that it can dry easily into a dry, stone-hard object. The drying paste balls are attached to each other on a chain and hung in an area where air circulates. Free-floating microbes in the air (*koji*) attach themselves to the balls. These balls are then placed in a cloth bag and kept in a warm place for 4 weeks. The greenish color of the fermenting molds changes color according to the length of time of the fermentation. The hard balls are then cracked open to determine how well they have dried. Should the mold be too thick, the balls are lightly rinsed to remove excess mold, then dried again.

A brine is prepared with salt and water which is 5 to 10 times the weight of the balls and of 15% salinity. The cracked balls are added to the brine and covered with a light cloth. A natural evaporation takes place which is the process of brewing, quick in the warm summer and slower in winter. The brewing of the bean paste, mold, salt and water takes from 1 to 3 months. The color of this home-brewed soy sauce is a dark tea color, not the black of commercial sauce which is colored with caramel.

During the brewing several whole dried hot red chilies are floated in the brew. The chilies inhibit the growth of undesirable microbes that could contaminate the sauce. Charcoal, which has been cleaned and dried, is added to the brew to clarify the sauce.

Finally, the brew is drained and filtered from one container to another. The brew is brought to a slow boil and strained while still hot into a dry storage jar. The soy sauce is now ready to use. The residue left behind when the brew is drained and filtered is a soy paste; this is utilized for another purpose.

SOYBEAN CURD: This is that marvelous Chinese invention, high in protein and eclectic in use, which was incorporated centuries ago into the cuisines of China, Japan, Indonesia, and Korea where it is known as *tubu*.

There are two types: Chinese curd is a firm square about 4 inches wide and 1 inch thick. The other type, Japanese soybean curd, is soft, creamy and about 2 inches thick. Koreans use both types.

SWEET POTATO and **SWEET POTATO VINE** (*Ipomoea batatas*): This is the supermarket sweet potato as well as those I have seen and eaten in Korea, China and Indonesia. Potatoes can have a light purple as well as light or dark beige skins. The flesh is beige colored, not the dark, rich orange of the yam. However, either type is acceptable for our use in the United States. It is sold in some Latin American shops as *batata*.

The tender ends of the sweet potato vines are edible and Koreans include them in soups and stir-fried dishes.

TREE EARS (*Auricularia polytricha*): Often called Cloud Ears. A black fungus that grows on decaying trees in the forest; used in Korean cooking. The thin, black fragments are soaked in water for 1 hour and expand to several times their original size. Tree ears are sold dried in plastic bags in Asian groceries. They are more important in soups and stews for texture since they do not have a great deal of flavor.

TUKBAEGE: A hard, round clay pot and cover that is used on top of the stove to cook soups and stews. The pots are commercially produced in several sizes from that for a single serving to larger sizes for small groups. Restaurants have many. They are a great convenience since they move from the gas or electric heating element directly to the table where the pots retain heat for many minutes.

Food in the Korean Day

Nothing is more effective for uncovering the eating habits of an unknown country than traveling by bus and perambulating on foot around the countryside. This is what I did in that enormously fascinating country of Korea, tasting, munching, sampling the food in homes, public markets, nightly street fairs, while I absorbed the culinary customs. Aside from being informative, it was great fun.

Breakfast, I found, can be a soup, rice, any of several side dishes, or anything else according to personal preference. If it is eaten at home the choice will differ from one person to another or from one family to another. If eaten in one of the breakfast restaurants that cater to those male breadwinners who prefer to eat on their way to work, it is usually a *tukbaege* of gruel.

One morning in Chonju, I chose to go to one of the breakfast restaurants on a whole street of breakfast restaurants, to sample this dish. The kitchen had a bank of stoves with 20 burners, each one covered with a simmering pot (a *tukbaege*, their all-purpose cooking pot) filled with a gruel. At the appropriate time a raw egg was broken into the gruel and it was carried to the table where the heat of the rice cooked the egg. A generous sprinkling of black pepper was the only seasoning. Tasty, but no substitute for a good cup of coffee.

I was happy to find that several American fast-food restaurants have sprung up in recent years, the most impressive of which was a Wendy's, just around the corner from my hotel in Seoul. This became my breakfast oasis, where I was served a good double coffee and milk in a paper cup, and a fried egg sandwich between two slices of excellent bread. It gave my digestive system a respite from the concentrated diet of the classic Korean foods with their hot chilies and garlic.

Lunch is the same as breakfast, with noodles, soups, side dishes, or anything one chooses. Working people will throng the small public restaurants where à la carte dishes are prepared and served rapidly. Tubu (tofu) in soups is a popular food when heavily seasoned with the denjang (preserved bean paste), chili powder (or flakes) that excite the taste buds. Koreans do not dawdle over lunch; a people with an overstimulated work ethic, they often eat and run.

Dinner is a family gathering where the women of the house prepare the meals, simple or complex, for the men who have been out at work all day. The food served depends on what the family can afford, and is served in family style. On a low, traditional rectangular table, kimchi and other side dishes are placed, and when everyone is seated, individual bowls of rice, perhaps with a mixture of barley or soybeans, and the hot entrées appear.

Sweets as such are not a part of the meal, but are kept for snacks or for ceremonial occasions, but a plain piece of uncooked fruit may be offered. Koreans do not drink wine or water with their meals. When they do serve a liquid, barley tea is the drink of choice. To serve friends on social occasions or at the end of a meal, the favorite drink is persimmon punch.

In older times before modish western clothes became popular, young ladies sat at the corners of the tables. The men and elders of the family would be seated on the floor along the sides and at the more comfortable ends of the highly polished tables. Now, standard chairs and tables are the style.

It is in the early hours of the evening that the main streets in the cities vibrate with activity, as the street-food people emerge with their offerings served from small carts with heating units (gas), or with simple baskets of a regional specialty. Snack food of classic Korean fare, and now more and more western foods such as the popular doughnuts, are also for sale; it becomes a social occasion as one stops and eats or walks and munches. I noticed in several cities a sign, "English Bakery," over a food shop that carried soft and sweet rolls, sliced white breads and nicely wrapped sandwiches. Young Koreans patronized this foreign outlet and I, too, longing for bread as a change from the ubiquitous white rice, carried out a bag of rolls to munch on as I strolled around town.

People relish the sociability as well as the considerable variety afforded them by this opportunity for noshing (and yet one never sees a fat Korean). It is so much more festive than going straight home from work!

The bulk of this book is devoted to recipes for the main meal, but in this chapter are just a few of special interest: a five-star breakfast, a ceremonial buckwheat cake, strings of date sweets for weddings, and the two drinks: barley tea and persimmon punch.

Kongnamul *Kuk Bap*

Chonju, an old city in southwest Korea, steeped in the history of the Yi dynasty, is celebrated for several dishes. This breakfast dish served in a *tukbaege* hot pot is one of them. The old south gate to the city is considered a national treasure and is now surrounded by the bustle of an active provincial capital. The marketplace, which I investigated on several occasions, is a large, sprawling building filled with clothes, housewares and every imaginable implement for the home and the farm. Dry fish, fruit, herbal medicines provide a mixture of olfactory sensations.

Outside along the banks of the river and stretching for many blocks were lady vendors in small shanty booths selling vegetables, chickens, fruit and an assortment of saltwater and freshwater fish.

Prominent were the long, 20- to 30-inch scallions tied in bundles and selling for pennies. The tofu vendors (all of them women) were selling large blocks of the soft variety with a design motif stamped in the top of each block. They were 30 cents each and large enough to enhance a good-size fish soup. Korean public markets hum with activity and good will.

A Korean breakfast does not follow the continental style of tea, toast and jam. It is much more important, sticks to the ribs, and is in itself a ritual of quantity and variety. Here is one breakfast that I ate at 8 A.M. in the port city of Pusan: A bowl of rice; bean curd and fish soup; fried egg; sea laver shreds; grilled fish; red bean stew; fermented kimchi; water kimchi; fish roe; beef shreds and green pepper; eggplant salad; and burdock (*Arctium lappa*) sauté, which is considered to be good for strength and endurance and is an aphrodisiac.

Here is a Chonju breakfast dish.

- **3/4 ..... CUP COOKED RICE**
- **1/4 ..... CUP BEAN SPROUTS, BLANCHED IN 2 CUPS BOILING WATER FOR 5 MINUTES**
- **1 ...... CUP HOT WATER RESERVED FROM THE BEAN SPROUTS**
- **1/4 ..... TEASPOON SALT**
- **1 ...... WHOLE EGG**
- **1 ...... TEASPOON TOASTED SESAME SEEDS**
- **1/2 TO 1 .. TEASPOON HOT RED CHILI POWDER**
- **1 ...... SCALLION, SLICED**
- **PINCH OF PEPPER**

1 Put the rice, bean sprouts, hot water and salt in a pan or in your own *tukbaege*. Break an egg over all, sprinkle with the sesame seeds, chili powder to taste, the scallion and pepper.

2 Put the pan (or *tukbaege*) on the gas flame and bring to a boil over moderate heat. Cook for 2 minutes but do not stir. Serve hot in bowls. The diner or the cook in the kitchen will break the egg yolk and mix everything in the pan into a gruel.

Serves 2, although 1 Korean could easily eat the entire portion.

NOTE: *There were 4 side dishes served with the gruel: cabbage kimchi, radish kimchi, salted baby shrimps and shreds of beef in soy sauce.*

Bori Cha

ROASTED, UNHULLED BARLEY WATER TEA

Koreans are not essentially tea drinkers like the Chinese or Japanese. Upon being seated in a Korean restaurant or home you are more than likely to be served a very pale-colored tea prepared from barley. This brew, which has a light earthy flavor, is considered to be a health tea, good for one's digestive system, especially if sipped after dining. I prefer to take the tea in small Chinese teacups at room temperature although it can be served quite warm or cooled in the refrigerator.

2 ..... TABLESPOONS UNHULLED BARLEY
5 ..... CUPS BOILING WATER

1 Put the barley in a large skillet and toast over moderate heat for about 10 minutes until the grains have turned to a dark coffee color. Stir and shake the pan now and then during this time. Set aside and cool.
2 Put the toasted barley into the boiling water and simmer over low heat for 15 to 20 minutes. Strain the mixture and discard the barley. Cool and serve at room temperature or refrigerate and serve when wanted.

Makes 5 cups.

Soo Jeung Kwa

PERSIMMON PUNCH

The first time I tasted this delectable treat was after a traditional Korean dinner in a restaurant where it was served ice cold in individual glass bowls. In each bowl, floating on top of the punch, were 3 pine nuts. Aromatic, with the pronounced flavor of fresh ginger and cinnamon, the punch had been sweetened to just the right intensity. The contrast between the hot chili-spiced entrées, the side dishes and the punch was astonishing and highly appropriate. It should always be served cold.

- 1 ...... **GALLON COLD WATER (4 QUARTS)**
- ¼ ..... **POUND FRESH GINGER, THOROUGHLY RINSED, SLICED THIN WITH THE SKIN**
- 2 ...... **OUNCES CINNAMON STICKS, ABOUT 8 TO 10 STICKS**
- 2 ...... **CUPS SUGAR, TO TASTE**
- 6 ...... **WHOLE SEMI-DRIED PERSIMMONS, CUT INTO 1-INCH TRIANGLES**

1 Bring the water to a boil with the ginger and cinnamon sticks. Cook over moderate heat for ½ hour. Strain the liquid and discard the ginger but leave the cinnamon in the punch.
2 Add the sugar while the liquid is still hot, to dissolve it. Add the persimmons to the lukewarm liquid and cool. The color of the punch becomes an old rose shade. Refrigerate the punch and serve cold.

Serve whenever wanted with any Asian food.

Makes 1 gallon.

NOTE: *The Korean persimmon (Diospyros kaki) used in the punch is the large, orange, egg-shaped type. It is eaten when fully ripe—very soft, orange-colored and with a creamy texture. In Korea, the unripe persimmons are picked in the autumn when the fruits are becoming ripe. The fruits are peeled and strung together but spaced like the lights on a Christmas tree. The strings of fruit are then attached to the persimmon tree to dry. Cool nights and warm days accelerate the drying, but during the week that it takes to dry, certain microbes that are floating freely in the garden air attach themselves to the peeled persimmons. After several days, the persimmons wilt and each one is then pushed together by hand to flatten on the drying string. When a white mold appears the fruit is dry enough to be packaged and sold, to be used in the punch.*
   This procedure is a good illustration of the Korean ingenuity used in preserving their seasonal fruits and vegetables. It may also explain why dried persimmons are so expensive and uncommon.

Pi Baek Daechu

Date Sweets

A Korean wedding, full of pageantry, symbolism and eternal vows, is the occasion when the Date Sweets are offered by the bride to the groom. The first red, ripened dates are harvested from the trees during September/October in Korea. A honey, sugar, and water syrup (or a barley malt syrup) is prepared with a dash of cinnamon as an aromatic touch. The whole dates are dipped into this treacle, then rolled in sesame seeds.

A chain of the dipped dates is prepared by sewing them together with needle and thread, each date being separated from the next by one pine nut that is threaded on the line. About 1 gallon of dates, many hundreds, are prepared this way and the chains deposited on a lacquer tray reserved for this purpose. The family symbol is branded on the bottom of the tray.

The bride presents the tray covered with a small mountain of the date chains to the family elders as an offering, and it joins wine and seasoned meats on the "bowing" or greeting table.

The elders then pull off handsful of the dates from the string and throw them at the traditionally gowned bride who is wearing a *jang ot* or wedding robe. (Much as we, in the West, throw rice.) This symbolic gesture is to celebrate health, prosperity and the birth of many children. Afterwards, on this most happy occasion, the guests eat the balance of the dates.

Sae Me Duk

STEAMED BUCKWHEAT CAKE

One of the museums in Cheju City on the island of Cheju has a wax dummy
of a buckwheat cake as one of the food exhibits. This represents a
steamed cake that was always served at ceremonials or on birthdays
in the past but is no longer used. Like so many traditional foods,
younger generations have lost interest in the symbolism and religious
significance of certain foods and this wax dummy may soon be the
only example left. This simple, unadorned cake is tasty, but the recipe
is included for historical purposes only.

2...... CUPS BUCKWHEAT FLOUR
¹/₂ ..... TEASPOON SALT
ABOUT ¹/₂ CUP WATER

1 Prepare a firm dough with the flour, salt and as much water as
necessary to create a manageable dough.
2 Roll out the dough into a ¼-inch-thick rectangle. Cut it into six
squares and put them on an oiled perforated tray in a Chinese style
steamer. Cook over moderate heat for 10 minutes.

Serve warm on special days.

Makes 6 cakes.

Kimchi

Korea's most celebrated dish—*kimchi*, their pickle—is instantly recognized as Korean even by those not familiar with the cuisine. Usually and erroneously, it is thought to be only a type of pickled cabbage full of garlic and hot chili. More accurately, the term covers fish, seafood, fruit and a large array of vegetables or any kind of botanical herb that is both edible and palatable. There are reputed to be about 200 kinds of kimchi.

The history of kimchi is about 2,000 years old, and the reverence that Koreans have for this indispensable and, they believe, life-giving concoction is almost mythical. Laborers building the Great Wall of China ate an early form of kimchi, and Genghis Khan was reputed to have fed some type of pickled cabbage to his troops.

During the sixteenth century, Koreans discovered that kimchi could also be prepared with vegetables other than the ubiquitous Asian cabbage. Eggplant, cucumbers, leeks, radishes, scallions, mixed with herbs and hot chili and leaves of the countryside, were incorporated into varieties of kimchi to provide many different flavors and textures. During the twentieth century newer vegetables not indigenous to Korea were added to the standard repertoire: carrots, tomatoes, Brussels sprouts and the European cabbage became welcome additions.

There is much more to kimchi than being the ever-present side dish of Korean meals. The herbs and spices, the hot chili, fresh ginger, garlic and salt act as natural preservatives for all the foods not available fresh in the nonproductive seasons of autumn and winter, and therefore kimchi provides a dependable source of food during the cold months.

Kimchi is partly responsible for one of the most distinctive sights in Korea—the thousands of black earthenware storage pots that are lined up on the flat rooftops of apartments and private homes, and are tucked away in corners of the house and buried in the garden for winter storage.

These pots, called *jahng dak*, have been made by Korean potters from the early days and are still available in various sizes of 5, 10, and up to 40 gallons.

(Another facet of the potters' art is the celadon—so exquisite that it was prized not only by Korean royal families but also by many beyond Korea's boundaries. This porcelain was a Chinese invention but highly refined by the Koreans. At one period, famous Korean potters were kidnapped by the occupying Japanese and taken to Japan where they were forced to teach Japanese potters their art.)

The black pots are still used to store kimchi for long-term preservation, and can be used for storage of other foods, as I have found. I have a pot bought in a pottery shop in Kyongju, shaped like a ginger jar, with a black glaze inside and out; it holds 1 gallon and is 8 inches high.

But to return to the kimchi, there is another type that has a short term of fermentation or can be eaten as a well-spiced fresh salad. Three days during summer or 1 week during cooler weather is enough fermentation prior to serving. Both types are represented among the following recipes.

The Seven Components of Kimchi

1 The chili taste, hot or sweet
2 Saltiness
3 Sweetness
4 Sourness
5 Bitterness
***6** Astringency
****7** Ingredient for intensifying or enhancing flavor

*Astringency is found in an unripe persimmon; it leaves a flavor on the palate like alum or tannin.

**The synthetic enhancer MSG artificially stimulates the taste buds but the same thing may be accomplished by using a natural food, for instance, toasted sesame seeds or seaweed.

Baechu Kimchi

CABBAGE PICKLE

Early one morning I was wandering around small side streets in Kyongju, a historical and beautiful city known as the "Museum without Walls." It was a bright, warm, sunny day and in front of a small grocery store two elderly ladies were preparing their kimchi on the sidewalk. As I watched, they sliced each cabbage from stem to stern, lengthwise, right through the core, into 4 or 6 equal pieces (depending on the size of cabbage). From a plastic dishpan they grabbed a handful of coarse salt and sprinkled it generously amongst the leaves.

Then they placed the cabbage in another larger pan where it would remain until it became limp—a process, the ladies told me through their English-speaking niece, that would take from 3 hours to overnight. At that point they rinsed the cabbage with cold water and firmly pressed out all excess liquid. The cabbage was then ready to be made into kimchi.

1	HEAD OF NAPA CABBAGE (2½ TO 3 POUNDS), HALVED LENGTHWISE
3	TABLESPOONS COARSE SALT
3	GARLIC CLOVES, CUT INTO JULIENNE STRIPS
1	TEASPOON JULIENNE STRIPS OF FRESH GINGER
6	SCALLIONS, CUT INTO 3-INCH PIECES
2	SCALLIONS, SLICED THIN
¼	POUND KOREAN RADISH, CUT INTO JULIENNE STRIPS
2	TABLESPOONS FISH SAUCE
3	TABLESPOONS HOT RED CHILI POWDER
3	TABLESPOONS HOT WATER
6 TO 8	ROUND SLICES OF KOREAN RADISH ¼-INCH THICK, PEELED

1 Sprinkle the salt all over the cabbage sections, lifting up some leaves to sprinkle inside. Let stand at room temperature for 3 hours in a dish large enough to hold the substantial amount of liquid that will accumulate. Then rinse the cabbage with cold water and firmly press out the liquid. Set aside.

2 To make the stuffing, mix together the garlic, ginger, all the scallions, julienned radish, fish sauce, chili powder and hot water. Toss the mixture as though it were a salad.

3 Take a handful of the stuffing and rub it all around the exterior of the two cabbage sections, scattering some between the leaves. Then take the outer green leaves of the cabbage still attached to the core and fold them over to enclose the stuffing.

4 Rub the round slices of radish with some of the stuffing and put them on the bottom of a large glass or plastic container with a tight lid. Put the cabbage over them and the remaining stuffing over all. Cover tightly. (I also put the jar in a plastic bag to prevent the pungent aroma from wafting around the kitchen and refrigerator.)

During the cool weather, let the kimchi mature at room temperature for 24 hours, then refrigerate for 5 days before tasting. In warm weather, put the kimchi directly into the refrigerator to mature. Serve after 3 days.

Makes 2 quarts.

Bosam Kimchi

The literal translation of Bosam Kimchi is "bag-wrapped cabbage pickle." The bag that gives this kimchi its name is made up of several cabbage leaves; a bundle is a more accurate definition of Bosam. It is a pickle using unusual (for a pickle) ingredients such as octopus, chestnuts, pine nuts and fish sauce. This excellent kimchi is usually prepared and served on special occasions. It is a fresh pickle, not one that has fermented for a long time as is true of the other types of kimchis; it can be served 3 to 4 days after preparation.

You will need a large-mouth glass or plastic container for these pickles—one that will hold at least 2 quarts.

2 ...... **POUNDS NAPA CABBAGE**

1 ...... **KOREAN RADISH, ABOUT 1 POUND**

½ ..... **GALLON COLD WATER**

3 ...... **OUNCES COARSE SALT**

1 ...... **TABLESPOON FISH SAUCE**

1 ...... **TABLESPOON DRIED HOT RED CHILI FLAKES**

2 ...... **GARLIC CLOVES, CHOPPED**

1 ...... **TEASPOON CHOPPED FRESH GINGER**

5 ...... **SCALLIONS, CUT INTO 1-INCH LENGTHS**

¼ ..... **POUND OCTOPUS, CUT INTO VERY THIN SLICES**

4 ...... **CHESTNUTS, PEELED, SLICED THIN**

1 ...... **TABLESPOON PINE NUTS**

1 ...... **TEASPOON DRIED RED CHILI THREADS**

1 Remove and reserve 8 large outer cabbage leaves. Cut the remainder of the cabbage horizontally into 1½-inch pieces. Set aside.
2 Cut the unpeeled radish into 1-inch cubes, then cut each cube into ¼-inch-thick slices.
3 Thoroughly mix the water and salt together. Put the sliced cabbage and radish in the glass or plastic container with the outer cabbage leaves on top. Pour enough of the brine over the vegetables to cover them, and weight the contents with a saucer to keep the vegetables under the brine. Leave overnight in a cool place to wilt. The next day drain it, discarding the brine. Set aside the outer cabbage leaves.
4 Mix together the fish sauce, chili flakes, garlic, ginger, scallions, octopus, chestnuts, pine nuts and red chili threads, then combine with the cabbage and radish pieces in a large bowl.

5 Place 4 wilted cabbage leaves on a plate, arranging them one across the other to cover it. Put half of the cabbage and radish mixture in the center of the leaves. Fold the leaves over the mixture to enclose the contents and place in the glass container with the folded leaves underneath. Do this for each bundle.

A certain amount of liquid will accumulate during the next day (the kimchi juice) but if not enough to cover the cabbage, add more liquid. (Mix 1 tablespoon fish sauce and 1 quart of water.) Pour this over the kimchi and put a plate over all to press the kimchi under the liquid to keep it from deteriorating.

The Bosam is best eaten 3 to 4 days after preparation. It should be stored in a cool place.

Makes 2 quarts.

Oie Sobaegi

STUFFED CUCUMBER PICKLE

A family-style pickle (kimchi) for daily dining, this is one of my favorites.

- 1 ...... **POUND KIRBY CUCUMBERS (4)**
- 3 ...... **TABLESPOONS SALT**
- 3 ...... **SCALLIONS, SLICED THIN**
- 1 ...... **SMALL ONION, CHOPPED (½ CUP)**
- 10 ..... **CHINESE CHIVES, CUT INTO 1-INCH PIECES**
- ¼ ..... **CUP DICED CARROT (¼-INCH DICE)**
- 1 ...... **TABLESPOON CHOPPED SALTED BABY SHRIMPS (SAEWOO JUT)**
- 1 ...... **TEASPOON CRUSHED GARLIC**
- 1 ...... **TEASPOON CRUSHED FRESH GINGER**
- 1 ...... **TABLESPOON HOT RED CHILI POWDER**
- 2 ...... **TABLESPOONS HOT WATER**

1 Cut each cucumber horizontally into halves. Make a cut in each piece lengthwise and crosswise 2 inches deep and press open, rubbing the salt inside and outside of each piece. Set aside for 1 hour while the pulp softens.

2 Prepare the stuffing. Mix together the scallions, onion, chives, carrot, shrimps, garlic, ginger, chili and hot water. Toss the stuffing as though it were a salad.

3 Rinse the cucumbers with cold water and drain well, shaking off excess liquid. Press open each piece and push in about 2 tablespoons of the stuffing. Rub some around the exterior of the cucumber. Place them in a glass or plastic container that has a tight lid. Add the remaining stuffing and liquid and tightly cover. (I also put it into a plastic bag so that the highly pungent aroma will not permeate the refrigerator.) Allow the kimchi to mature at room temperature for 24 hours before serving. Always refrigerate after opening.

NOTE: *Kimchi at room temperature undergoes the very slightest fermentation during the maturation period. This enhances the flavor but also dilutes the chili intensity somewhat. The quantity of chili powder may seem to be excessive but in reality it blends smoothly into the other flavors.*

Kaji Kimchi

It is the long, slender oriental eggplant found throughout Asia (and in Asian Shopping Districts) that is used by the Koreans to produce this, one of the favorite kimchis. There are two methods of making this pickle: the eggplant may be lightly cooked and stuffed or, for a stronger-flavored pickle with a firm texture, it may be pickled raw (see Variation). The indispensable dried hot red chili flakes provide the fire. Not for the timid.

2 ...... CUPS WATER

1 ...... POUND ORIENTAL EGGPLANTS (ABOUT 2)

1 ...... TEASPOON SALT

1 ...... SEMI-HOT GREEN CHILI, SEEDED, CUT INTO 3-INCH-LONG JULIENNE STRIPS

2 ...... GARLIC CLOVES, CRUSHED

1 ...... INCH OF FRESH GINGER, CRUSHED

2 ...... SCALLIONS, CUT INTO 3-INCH-LONG STRIPS, THE WHITE PART QUARTERED

2 ...... TEASPOONS HOT RED CHILI FLAKES

3 ...... TABLESPOONS JULIENNE STRIPS OF ONION, CHINESE CHIVE, OR KOREAN RADISH

1 Bring the water, eggplants and salt to a boil in a saucepan large enough to contain all the ingredients. Cook over moderate heat for 3 minutes, turning the eggplant in the water now and then. The eggplant should be half-cooked and pliant but not mushy. Remove and set aside, cool, and cut into 3 equal pieces. Cut a deep cross in one end of each piece so that they can be opened and stuffed. Set aside.

2 Thoroughly mix the green chili, garlic, ginger, scallions, chili flakes and onion or chive or radish together. Open up the cut in each eggplant and push in about 2 tablespoons of the stuffing. Place the stuffed eggplant in a glass or plastic container that has a tight cover. Cover the container and put it in a cool but not refrigerated spot for 1 day to mature. Then serve and refrigerate. The kimchi is best eaten during the first 3 days if you prefer a light flavor but for more bite, wait until later in the week when the mixture will have fermented. It can be refrigerated for a maximum of 1 week.

Makes 1 quart.

(Continued next page)

VARIATION: *There are some who prefer their eggplant pickle to be freshly firm in texture with more chili strength. For those people the eggplant can be prepared the same way as the half-cooked version with several simple changes.*

Cut each uncooked eggplant into 3 equal parts. Make a deep crosscut in one end of each piece. Then, using coarse salt, salt each piece liberally, inside and out, spreading open the incision to do so. Let stand for ½ hour. Rinse the pieces under cold water and dry well on kitchen towels.

Then proceed to stuff as in regular recipe and store in a cool place for 24 hours. The uncooked version of the eggplant kimchi may be refrigerated for up to 1 week or a bit longer. Longer is stronger.

Kaktugi Kimchi

Koreans like the taste of this popular kimchi but also believe that it is "very good for the stomach." The word *Kaktugi* indicates that this radish has been cut into chunks. It is the Korean or Chinese radish (*Raphanus sativus*), the top of which is a murky green, the bottom part (the taproot) is white. It may have a few straggly leaves attached to the top, which are edible.

During the winter, this pickle is stored in the jet-black pots called *jahng dak*. Farmers dig holes in the earth to fit large jars of kimchi, and there they are protected from the intense cold but provided with enough refrigeration to preserve the pickle for the winter's supply of vitamins, flavoring and solace for the stomach.

1 ...... **POUND KOREAN RADISH, PEELED, CUT INTO 1-INCH CUBES**

3 ...... **SCALLIONS OR THE EQUIVALENT IN CHINESE CHIVES, CUT INTO 2-INCH LENGTHS**

1 ...... **HEAD OF GARLIC (ABOUT 12 CLOVES), PEELED AND CHOPPED**

1 ...... **INCH OF FRESH GINGER, CHOPPED**

3 OR 4 ... **TABLESPOONS HOT RED CHILI POWDER, TO TASTE**

1 ...... **TABLESPOON FINE-CHOPPED SALTED TINY SHRIMPS**

½ ...... **TEASPOON SALT**

1 ...... **TEASPOON SUGAR**

Mix everything together and store in a glass or pottery container with a tight cover. Allow to ferment for 24 hours, then refrigerate. It is ready to eat immediately but it may be stored in the refrigerator for several months.

Serve with any kind of Korean food as a side dish.

Makes 1 quart.

Chong Kak Kimchi

YOUNG BACHELOR RADISH PICKLE

Actually, this is the young white Korean radish with a flutter of leaves attached to the stem end. The title compares a developing radish, not quite mature but still white and tender, to a bachelor. This is an intermediary stage of the radish growth.

2	**POUNDS YOUNG KOREAN RADISH, 2 TO 3 INCHES LONG**
¼	**CUP PLUS 1 TEASPOON SALT**
2	**CUPS WATER**
2	**TABLESPOONS FLOUR**
3	**SCALLIONS, SHREDDED INTO THIN 3-INCH-LONG PIECES**
1	**WHOLE HEAD OF GARLIC, THE CLOVES PEELED AND CHOPPED**
1	**INCH OF FRESH GINGER, CHOPPED**
1	**TEASPOON SUGAR**
1	**TABLESPOON FINE-CHOPPED TINY SALTED SHRIMPS**
3 TO 4	**TABLESPOONS HOT RED CHILI POWDER, TO TASTE**

1 Peel the radish and cut into 2-inch pieces (or they may be small enough to halve). Trim the leaves. Rinse them and the radish in cold water, then toss with ¼ cup salt and let stand for 1 hour. Rinse with cold water and drain.

2 Bring the water and flour to a boil, stirring continuously to blend and dissolve flour. Cool well. Mix in the radish and all the vegetables, 1 teaspoon salt, the sugar, chopped shrimps and chili powder. Pack the mixture into a glass jar with a tight cover and let stand at room temperature for 1 day to mature. Then refrigerate and serve when wanted.

Makes 2 quarts.

NOTE: *My Korean chef says that the mixture of water and flour prevents a too strong aroma emanating from the kimchi.*

Yul Mu Kimchi

The white (Korean) radish is so ubiquitous in Korean dining that it is missed when it does not appear on the table as a side dish or in some other guise. I first tasted this particular pickle with a chicken dish (Samgyetang) at a restaurant on Cheju Island, where the owner had the cook demonstrate to me how it was prepared.

1 ...... **POUND KOREAN RADISH**
2 ...... **CUPS COLD WATER**
2 ...... **TEASPOONS SALT**
1 ...... **TEASPOON SUGAR**
1 ...... **WHOLE FRESH HOT GREEN CHILI**

1 Peel the radish and rinse in cold water, then cut it into sticks 2 inches long by ½ inch thick.
2 Mix the water, salt and sugar together, add the radish and chili, and store in a glass or pottery jug with a cover. Leave at room temperature for 2 to 3 days to ferment slightly.

Serve with any kind of Korean food and refrigerate thereafter.

Serves 6 or more.

Yoel Mu Mul Kimchi

PICKLED YOUNG RADISH LEAVES

In the spring, when the green leaves sprout from the Korean radish (*Raphanus sativus*) it is time to prepare the kimchi. In fact, the various stages of development of the radish from the emerging leaves to the young root and finally the mature root, are all utilized in separate preparations of the kimchi. Each one has its own texture and flavor even though the seasonings may be similar.

1½ ..... POUNDS YOUNG RADISH LEAVES, CUT INTO 2-INCH PIECES

3 ...... SCALLIONS, SHREDDED THIN

1 ...... HEAD OF GARLIC, THE CLOVES PEELED AND SHREDDED

1 ...... INCH OF FRESH GINGER, SHREDDED

2 ...... FRESH WHOLE SEMI-HOT CHILIES (1 RED AND 1 GREEN), EACH CUT INTO 5 DIAGONAL SLICES

1 ...... TABLESPOON SALT, OR TO TASTE

1 ...... TABLESPOON SUGAR

2 ...... CUPS WATER

Mix all the vegetables together in a large bowl. Dissolve the salt and sugar in the water and pour this over the vegetables. Mix well and store in a glass jar with a tight cover. Keep at room temperature for 1 day to mature and then store in the refrigerator. The kimchi is ready to eat.

May be stored in the refrigerator for 2 months.

Makes 2 quarts.

Mul Kimchi

This is called a pickle but the large amount of water in it makes it more of
a cold and refreshing soup. The radish develops a slightly fermented
flavor and the garlic and chili furnish the underlying authority. Koreans
are very partial to garlic and sometimes overdo its use. One could
reduce the amount used here without losing any of the character or
authenticity of the pickle. When dining in Korean restaurants, the
Mul Kimchi is frequently one of the side dishes offered automatically
as part of the meal.

1 ...... **POUND OF RADISH, PEELED**
4 ...... **GARLIC CLOVES, CHOPPED FINE**
2 ...... **TEASPOONS SUGAR**
3 ...... **CUPS WATER**
1 ...... **SCALLION, CUT INTO 2-INCH PIECES**
1 ...... **SWEET RED PEPPER, CUT INTO
JULIENNE STRIPS (1 CUP)**
6 TO 8 .. **DRIED HOT RED CHILI THREADS**

1 Cut the radish into 1-inch-square pieces, ½ inch thick. Mix them
with the garlic and sugar and put them into a glass jar. Let stand for
½ hour.
2 Add the water and mix well. Then add the scallion, red pepper and
chili threads. Cover the jar and let stand at room temperature for 2
days during which it becomes lightly fermented. The red pepper and
chili provide the color and some flavor.

Then refrigerate the jar, tightly covered, and serve with Korean food.
Both the radish and liquid are served together in a small bowl.

Makes about 1 quart.

Seuck Bak Ji

MIXED VEGETABLES AND COD KIMCHI

Cod is a winter fish, eaten during the months when ice, snow and frigid winds blow down from Manchuria into the Korean peninsula. But in Korea cod is also expensive, possibly more so than beef, and Koreans take that into consideration when using it. Being health-conscious, they consider all the advantages of combining the protein-rich cod with the vitamin-rich (and cheaper) vegetables to come up with this luscious tongue-tingling kimchi.

You will need a gallon jar with a tight cover for this recipe.

2 ...... **POUNDS FRESH CODFISH, CUT INTO 2-INCH SQUARES, 1 INCH THICK**

6 ...... **TABLESPOONS COARSE SALT**

2 ...... **POUNDS NAPA CABBAGE**

1 ...... **POUND KOREAN RADISH**

8 ...... **SCALLIONS, CUT INTO 1 ½-INCH LENGTHS**

1 ...... **INCH OF FRESH GINGER, PEELED, SLICED THIN**

4 ...... **GARLIC CLOVES, SLICED THIN**

3 ...... **TABLESPOONS DRIED HOT RED CHILI FLAKES**

1 ...... **TABLESPOON FISH SAUCE**

1 ...... **CUP WATER**

1 Sprinkle the cod pieces with 2 tablespoons salt. Mix gently. Put in a glass or pottery bowl, cover and refrigerate overnight. A substantial amount of liquid may accumulate. Drain the fish and set aside in a large mixing bowl.
2 Remove the green outer leaves of the cabbage and reserve them for another use. Cut the inner white leaves into 1½-inch lengths. Cut the radish into thin pieces 2 inches by 1 inch. Mix the cabbage and radish together with 4 tablespoons salt in a large mixing bowl. Cover and refrigerate overnight. Drain the liquid that has accumulated.
3 Now gently mix together the cabbage, radish and cod. Add the scallions.

4 In a blender, process together the ginger, garlic, chili flakes, fish sauce and water until smooth. Pour this over the vegetables and cod and mix together. Put everything into a gallon glass or pottery container. Weigh the contents down with a saucer.

Allow 2 days at room temperature to ferment. After 1 day turn the mixture over in the jar, then refrigerate the container or place it in a cool cellar. Let the fermentation process continue for 2 weeks before using. The microbes that provide the fermentation produce the characteristic flavor of the kimchi.

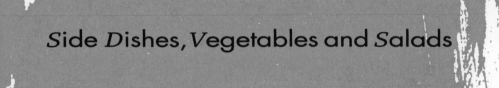

Side Dishes, Vegetables and Salads

One of the principal characteristics of Korean dining and certainly one of the most attractive is the presentation of all the side dishes that are placed on the table, whether at home or in a restaurant, as one waits for the expected entrées. Side dishes, in 3-inch plates or bowls, are brought to the table automatically; the generosity of the host is reflected by the number of dishes offered.

A minimum number would be five, anything less would leave large blank spaces on the table and this is to be avoided. Any variety of kimchi could be included as a side dish as well as vegetables, salads, pickled squid or crab, or a light and refreshing cold soup to cool the palate. The quantity, quality and variety depend upon the preference of the home cook or restaurant chef. The ingenuity of the cook is called upon to produce a multitude of side dishes, all of which are compatible with Korean culinary tradition and with the dishes that are to follow.

The side dishes are served first as the guests sit on the floor at the low Korean dining tables or at the standard Western table. Sometimes this includes a small cup of barley tea which can be sipped while waiting for the major dishes. The side dishes function as appetizers as the guests nibble along, using the slender silver chopsticks or the plain, short bamboo throw-away type, while awaiting the more important foods.

Good Korean beer and saki make their appearance if requested as the guests await the main entrées. A basket of greens consisting of chrysanthemum leaves, lettuce and tender Napa cabbage leaves is usually served with the side dishes. The greens are used as wrappers for either barbecued meats or without a filling but slathered with fermented bean paste and hot sauces, rolled up like cigars and eaten as an accompaniment to drinks, rice or whatever appeals to the diner.

No grease, oils or artificial seasonings are included to refute the Korean mania for the march of health through food.

Chaban

The word *Chaban* encompasses this trio of side dishes that seem to belong
together. It is the custom in some families to serve these three in a
three-section glass or porcelain container at every meal. They are
prepared separately, although with the same marinade, and of
course could be served separately, if desired.

The dried flying fish and anchovies are sold in Asian groceries
where they are found neatly packed in plastic bags.

For the Marinade:

½ ..... CUP SOY SAUCE
1 ...... TABLESPOON GOCHU JANG
2 ...... TABLESPOONS SUGAR
1 ...... TEASPOON TOASTED SESAME SEEDS
1 ...... TEASPOON KOREAN SESAME OIL
3 ...... SCALLIONS, SLICED THIN

1 ...... CUP SMALL DRIED ANCHOVIES
1 ...... CUP DRIED FLYING FISH
1 ...... CUP THIN SLICES OF BEEFSTEAK,
         3 INCHES LONG

1 Mix together the soy sauce, gochu jang, sugar, sesame seeds, sesame
oil and scallions to make the marinade. Mix with the dried anchovies
and set aside.
2 Prepare the same marinade and mix with the flying fish. Set aside.
3 Mix another batch of the marinade for the beef slices and put them
into a small pan with a cover. Simmer over low heat for 10 to 15 minutes, or until the meat is tender.

Serve as side dishes. They can be stored separately in glass jars in the
refrigerator for several weeks.

Makes 1 cup of each.

Myulchi Boekum

DRIED ANCHOVY CONDIMENT

Dried anchovies play an important role in Korean cooking. The large size, 2 or 3 inches, are soaked in water for a lengthy period and then discarded, reserving the broth (or anchovy water), which is used as a basis for soups. The smaller size, from ½ to 1 inch, are seasoned and used as a condiment or side dish. Almost automatically, this dish is served in restaurants and homes to diners who crave the sweet, hot and chewy qualities of the anchovies. The standard chili-hot seasoning paste known as gochu jang provides the strong red color. Note that there is no salt added since the anchovies retain their natural sea salt.

3 ...... TEASPOONS CORN OIL

2 ...... GARLIC CLOVES, CRUSHED

½ ..... CUP DRIED ANCHOVIES, 1 TO 1½ INCHES LONG

2 ...... TEASPOONS SOY SAUCE

1 ...... TEASPOON GOCHU JANG

2 ...... SCALLIONS, SLICED THIN

1 ...... TEASPOON SUGAR

½ ..... TEASPOON KOREAN SESAME OIL

½ ..... TEASPOON SESAME SEEDS

1 Put the oil in a skillet, add the garlic, and stir-fry over low heat for a few seconds. Add the anchovies and mix well. Add the soy sauce and stir-fry for 1 minute to ensure that the mix is uniform. Add the gochu jang in the center of the skillet and mix.

2 Add the scallions and sugar and stir-fry for 1 minute, mixing and tossing. Stir in the sesame oil and seeds and remove from the heat. Serve at room temperature with any Korean food.

Makes ½ cup.

Marun Panchan

There are not many sweet flavors on the Korean table. Most are salty, chili-hot or sometimes neutral—to be mixed with other elements. This recipe offers a combination of salt and sweet, with a chewy texture. It provides a contrast with the main dishes and other side dishes during a meal. It is one of my favorite side dishes since it surprises the palate when least expected. (It is slightly sweeter than the previous recipe.)

2 ...... TEASPOONS CORN OIL
3 ...... TEASPOONS SUGAR
1 ...... TEASPOON SOY SAUCE
1 ...... GARLIC CLOVE, CRUSHED
1/4 ..... INCH SLICE OF FRESH GINGER, CRUSHED
1/2 ..... TEASPOON GOCHU JANG
1 ...... CUP DRIED ANCHOVIES, 1-INCH LENGTH
2 ...... TEASPOONS TOASTED SESAME SEEDS

1 Heat the oil in a wok or skillet. Add the sugar, soy sauce, garlic, ginger and gochu jang all at once. Stir-fry over low heat for 1 minute.
2 When the mixture bubbles, add the anchovies and stir rapidly for about 1/2 minute to coat each anchovy with the seasonings. Stir in the sesame seeds, remove from the heat, and turn out into a small dish.

Serve cool or at room temperature with any kind of Korean food.

Makes 1/2 cup.

Sogogi Jangjolim

BEEF SHREDS IN SOY SAUCE

Although this is a side dish usually served with the principal meal, I had it the first time for breakfast. It was in Pusan, Korea's largest port, where I was served an elaborate breakfast of at least 12 dishes; this was one of the best. It has an unusual flavor for Korean food, with a predominantly chili-hot soy taste.

2 ...... CUPS WATER

½ ..... POUND BONELESS BEEF CHUCK OR STEAK

4 ...... GARLIC CLOVES, SLICED LENGTHWISE INTO 3 PIECES EACH

½ ..... TEASPOON SUGAR

4 ...... TABLESPOONS SOY SAUCE

1 OR 2 ... FRESH SEMI-HOT GREEN CHILIES, SLICED THIN, RINSED UNDER COLD WATER TO REMOVE SEEDS, DRAINED

1 Bring the water and beef to a boil in a pan over moderate heat and cook until tender, about 40 minutes. Cool the beef and reserve ½ cup of beef stock. Pull apart the beef into 3-inch-long shreds. Set aside.
2 Put the beef stock in a pan, add the garlic, sugar, soy sauce, and beef and simmer, covered, over low heat for 20 minutes. Stir in the chili, simmer for 1 minute more, and remove from the heat. Cool and refrigerate.

Serves 6 as a side dish.

Salmun Dalgyal Fey

HARD-COOKED EGG FLOWER

What an interesting invention, a simple multicolored design, and yet edible. This was an old family recipe—quite possibly a whimsical invention of the old grandmother.

- **6 ...... EGGS, AT ROOM TEMPERATURE**
- **2 ...... TABLESPOONS SOY SAUCE**
- **1 ...... TABLESPOON CRUSHED SESAME SEEDS**
- **1 ...... TEASPOON KOREAN SESAME OIL**
- **1 ...... CUP SHREDDED KOREAN RADISH OR CARROT, SOAKED IN COLD WATER FOR 1/2 HOUR**
- **PARSLEY OR CHRYSANTHEMUM LEAVES**
- **SEVERAL FRESH OR CANNED CHERRIES**

1 Cover the eggs with water and cook for 15 minutes. Drain and peel.

2 As soon as peeled, while still warm, hold one egg at a time between the thumb and forefinger and press gently to flatten the large end of the egg. On the other end, the thumb pressure will create a small depression. Cool the eggs.

3 Mix together the soy sauce, sesame seeds and oil to make the dip.

4 Drain the radish or carrot well and dry lightly on paper towels. Scatter the shreds (or short julienne strips) on a serving platter. Place the eggs flat side down in a circle with one in the center to form the flower. The shreds will support the eggs in an upright position. Put several leaves and 1 cherry in the depression at the top of the egg. Serve the platter with the dip on the side. Each diner will take an egg, quarter it and use as much of the dip as wanted.

Serve as an appetizer.

Serves 6 as a side dish.

NOTE: *It is very important that the eggs are warm and flexible so they can be squeezed and molded. If the eggs are cold they will break when pressure is applied.*

Keran Jchim

STEAMED EGG LOAF

It may be difficult to imagine a naturally neutral Korean dish that does not contain any hot chili. This steamed egg loaf is an attractive adjunct to a dinner that contains a variety of spiced dishes. It may be eaten hot, at room temperature, or if preferred on a hot day, cold and sliced.

1 ...... MEDIUM-SIZE ONION, CHOPPED ($\frac{1}{2}$ CUP)

1 ...... SMALL CARROT, CUT INTO $\frac{1}{8}$-INCH DICE ($\frac{1}{3}$ CUP)

$\frac{1}{2}$ ..... CUP WATER

2 ...... EGGS, LIGHTLY BEATEN

$\frac{1}{4}$ ..... POUND GROUND BEEF

1 ...... SCALLION, SLICED THIN WITH THE WHITE PART HALVED, THEN SLICED

$\frac{1}{2}$ ..... TEASPOON SALT, OR TO TASTE

$\frac{1}{4}$ ..... TEASPOON PEPPER

Mix everything together. Put the mixture into an oblong, heatproof 1-quart dish. Steam in a Chinese-style steamer over moderate heat for 40 minutes, or test with a chopstick for doneness.

Usually served warm.

Serves 4 with other dishes.

NOTE: *To test the loaf, after about 25 minutes plunge the end of a chopstick carefully into the center of the loaf. If the hole fills with liquid, more minutes are needed for a firmer texture. On the other hand, you may prefer, as some do, a soft, looser consistency, in which case the loaf is ready.*

Soonday

STUFFED SAUSAGE

In a number of cultures cooks stuff the small intestine of the cow, sheep or pig and boil, bake or roast it. In Tunisia, this is known as *merguez*; in Eastern Europe as *kishke*; in Indonesia, it is the spectacular *usus* in coconut milk. The *soonday* of Korea is entirely different.

It originated in the cold climate of mountainous North Korea where the intestines of the wild mountain pigs were used. Now it's prepared all over the country and brought in large buckets to the public markets of Pusan, Kyongu, Seoul, Taegu and elsewhere. This sausage stuffing is made of rice, seasonings and beef or pork blood (or tomato purée).

The cleaned intestine (beef or pork) may be found at your local butcher, especially Jewish and Italian shops where traditional foods are catered to.

1	**YARD OF SMALL BEEF INTESTINE**
2	**CUPS RICE, COOKED BY THE STANDARD METHOD BUT STILL SLIGHTLY FIRM**
2	**GARLIC CLOVES, CRUSHED**
¼	**INCH SLICE OF FRESH GINGER, CRUSHED**
1	**TEASPOON SALT**
½	**TEASPOON BLACK OR WHITE PEPPER**
1	**TABLESPOON KOREAN SESAME OIL**
1	**TEASPOON CRUSHED SESAME SEEDS**
5	**SCALLIONS, CHOPPED**
2	**CUPS BEEF OR PORK BLOOD (OPTIONAL), OR SUBSTITUTE 8 OUNCES CANNED TOMATO PURÉE**

1 Clean the intestine as received from your butcher once again. Rinse well in cold water, then soak in lightly salted water for 1 hour; this makes the intestine firm and easier to handle. Tie up one end firmly with cotton string.

2 Prepare the stuffing. Mix the cooked rice, garlic, ginger, salt, pepper, sesame oil, sesame seeds, scallions and either blood or tomato purée. Loosely stuff the intestine either by machine or by a funnel—forcing the stuffing along the entire length. Do not fill too tightly since the intestine may split in cooking when the rice expands. Tie the open end firmly.

The intestine may also be stuffed as individual sausages in which case it is cut into the desired lengths, tied, filled and tied again.

(Continued next page)

3 Place the *soonday* in a large pan, curling it around like a snail. Cover it with lightly salted water and bring to a boil. Then turn to low and cook *uncovered* for ¾ hour. At the end of this time, insert a skewer in the *soonday* to test for doneness. As when testing a cake, if the skewer is dry and the *soonday* is firm to pressure, it is done.

Cut diagonally into ¼-inch thick slices and serve warm or at room temperature (warm is better). Serve on festive occasions especially after the harvest of rice, cabbage (or whatever is being grown) with your favorite Korean dip.

Serves 6 to 8.

Kaji Namul

There is no end to the variety of vegetables that can be prepared as side dishes, depending upon the season and the vegetables available in the marketplace. What Shakespeare calls "all the good gifts of nature" are appropriate words for *namuls*. This side dish is prepared from the miniature eggplant always available in the supermarkets.

1 ...... POUND BABY EGGPLANTS (4)
1 ...... TABLESPOON SOY SAUCE
1 ...... TEASPOON KOREAN SESAME OIL
1 ...... TEASPOON TOASTED SESAME SEEDS
1 ...... GARLIC CLOVE, CRUSHED
⅛ ..... TEASPOON PEPPER
¼ ..... TEASPOON SUGAR
2 ...... TABLESPOONS CHOPPED CHINESE CHIVES OR SCALLIONS

1 Hold the eggplant so that the stem part is down and cut 4 crosscuts from the end almost to the stem, making 8 fingers. Do not cut all the way through, the 8 fingers are connected. Bring about 4 cups of lightly salted water to a boil, drop the eggplants in, and cook uncovered over moderate heat for about 5 minutes, or until they have become tender but with a touch of firmness. Drain well.
2 While the eggplants are still warm, cut off the stem which will release the 8 sections. Set aside.
3 Mix together the soy sauce, sesame oil, sesame seeds, garlic, pepper and sugar. Add the eggplant strips and toss well. Garnish with the chives or scallions. These are best eaten on the day of preparation.

Serve at room temperature.

Serves 6 as a side dish.

Goguma

BOILED SWEET POTATOES

Sweet potatoes are a popular side dish in restaurants and homes, and are frequently eaten as a snack by farmers working in the fields. They fill the need for a tasty and satisfying food at any time. Sweet potatoes were introduced into Korea from Japan in the eighteenth century to ward off threatening famine and soon became familiar throughout the country.

The potatoes are boiled in their skins until tender and are served at room temperature, usually cut into halves or quarters. They are or could be a rice substitute but in any event are a tasty morsel any way one would want them. I always looked forward to being served the sweet potato as a side dish in restaurants in Korea.

Muu Namul

The appearance of this side dish is important. Soy sauce, so often included with radishes to provide additional flavor, is omitted here. It would discolor the fresh white pulp of the radish and be uninviting. Salt is used instead.

- 1 ...... **POUND KOREAN RADISH, PEELED**
- 1 ...... **TEASPOON KOREAN SESAME OIL**
- 1 ...... **TEASPOON TOASTED SESAME SEEDS**
- ½ ..... **TEASPOON SALT**
- 1 ...... **GARLIC CLOVE, CRUSHED**
- ¼ ..... **TEASPOON SUGAR**
- ⅛ ..... **TEASPOON PEPPER**

Cut the radish into 3-inch-long pencil-thin sticks. Heat the oil in a skillet and stir-fry the radish over moderate heat for 1 minute to soften. Sprinkle with sesame seeds, salt, garlic, sugar and pepper; mix well for about ½ minute. Turn out into a serving dish.

Serve at room temperature as a side dish with Korean foods.

Serves 6 or more.

Hobak Namul

This is a very simple method of preparing zucchini and could be used for practically any vegetable of your choice.

3 ...... SMALL ZUCCHINI, ABOUT 1 POUND
1 ...... TEASPOON KOREAN SESAME OIL
1 ...... TEASPOON TOASTED SESAME SEEDS
1 ...... TABLESPOON SOY SAUCE
1 ...... GARLIC CLOVE, CRUSHED
¼ ..... TEASPOON SUGAR
⅛ ..... TEASPOON PEPPER

1 Cut the zucchini across into ⅛-inch-thick slices. Drop the slices into boiling water for ½ minute and rinse quickly under cold water. Drain and dry on a kitchen towel.
2 Mix together the sesame oil, sesame seeds, soy sauce, garlic, sugar and pepper. Toss the mixture well with the softened zucchini.

Serve at room temperature as a side dish with Korean food.

Serves 6 or more.

Tubu Choerim

FRIED SPICED BEAN CURD

Bean curd is not only nutritious as a meat substitute, but lends itself to various other uses. The Koreans fry bean-curd slices, season them with hot chili and garlic among other things, and transform an essentially bland food into one with distinctive flavor and a chewy texture.

3	**SOFT BEAN-CURD SQUARES, SLICED ½ INCH THICK**
	SALT, TASTE
3	**TABLESPOONS CORN OIL**
3	**TABLESPOONS SOY SAUCE**
3	**TABLESPOONS WATER**
1½ TO 2	**TEASPOONS HOT RED CHILI POWDER, TO TASTE**
1	**TEASPOON SESAME SALT**
1	**GARLIC CLOVE, CRUSHED TO A PASTE**
4	**SCALLIONS, CUT INTO 2-INCH PIECES**
ABOUT 20	**DRIED CHILI THREADS (OPTIONAL BUT TRADITIONAL)**

1 Dry the bean-curd slices on paper towels, then very lightly sprinkle a few grains of salt on one side of each slice. Let stand for 10 minutes. Heat the oil in a skillet and brown the slices over moderate heat for about 3 minutes on each side. Drain on paper towels.

2 Mix the soy sauce, water, chili powder, sesame salt, garlic and a few scallions together in a bowl. Put 1 tablespoon of the sauce and scallions on the bottom of a pan. Cover this with the bean-curd slices; sprinkle with sauce and several red chili threads. Add another layer of bean curd, more threads and sauce and continue until all the bean curd and sauce is used. Spread a few more chili threads on the top. Rinse the sauce bowl with 2 tablespoons water and pour it over all.

3 Bring the liquid to a boil, cover the pan and simmer over low heat for 15 minutes to steam through the curd slices. Most of the liquid will evaporate.

Serve warm with rice and salads for a vegetarian meal or with meat and fish dishes.

Serves 4.

Tubu Gui

STUFFED SOYBEAN CURD

Tubu is the Korean word for soybean curd (cake); *tofu* is the word used by the Chinese and Japanese, and the Indonesians call it *tahu*. Whatever word you use to describe this remarkable, high-protein food, the curd used here is the thick, soft style. It is not the firm square cube used in Chinese cooking.

- **4 ...... SOFT SOYBEAN CAKES (TUBU)**
- **¼ ..... POUND GROUND BEEF**
- **1 ...... GARLIC CLOVE, CRUSHED**
- **½ ..... INCH OF FRESH GINGER, CRUSHED**
- **2 ...... TABLESPOONS CHOPPED ONION**
- **¼ ..... TEASPOON BLACK PEPPER**
- **½ ..... TEASPOON SALT, PLUS A FEW GRAINS FOR SPRINKLING**
- **1 ...... TABLESPOON SOY SAUCE**
- **1 ...... TEASPOON KOREAN SESAME OIL**
- **CORN OIL FOR PANFRYING**
- **1 ...... TABLESPOON CHOPPED PARSLEY OR FINE-CHOPPED CHIVES**

1 Place the soybean curd on the cutting board and cut each one horizontally into 4 equal parts. Cut a 1-inch pocket in the center of each piece deep enough to contain 1 teaspoon stuffing.

2 Mix together the ground beef, garlic, ginger, onion, pepper, salt, soy sauce and sesame oil. Mix and mash well into a smooth consistency. Stuff 1 teaspoon of the mixture into each pocket. Sprinkle a few grains of the extra salt around the *tubu* but not on the pocket which is already seasoned.

3 Heat about 1 tablespoon corn oil in a skillet and fry each piece of stuffed *tubu* over high heat quickly on both sides. The color of the slices should be golden, not dark brown.

Serve warm with traditional Korean side dishes. Garnish the stuffed curd with parsley or chives.

Serves 4 to 6.

Gochu Muchim

Koreans have no fear of the hot chili whether green or red. Chilies (gochu) are prepared in many ways in this cuisine as befits these chili addicts. Here is a powerful side dish, a condiment with considerable flavor.

The semi-hot chili used here is known as the "elephant trunk" in India since it is shaped and curved like one.

¼ ..... POUND FRESH SEMI-HOT GREEN CHILI
½ ..... TEASPOON SALT
2 ...... TABLESPOONS FLOUR
1 ...... TEASPOON KOREAN SESAME OIL
1 ...... TEASPOON TOASTED SESAME SEEDS

1 Toss the chili, salt and flour together. Put them on a heatproof dish and steam in a Chinese-style steamer for about 20 minutes, or until quite tender.
2 Cool the chili, then toss with the sesame oil and seeds.

Serve at room temperature as a side dish with other Korean food.

Serves 6 as a side dish.

Kaji Sun

STUFFED EGGPLANT

The Kaji Sun is made in autumn when the eggplant flavor is at its best. The Koreans say that this preparation is for older people who have trouble with their teeth and therefore want food they do not have to chew very much. Actually, it is the flavor that counts. The skin of the long, narrow Asian eggplant is colored an intense purple—much darker than any I have seen in New York.

½ ...... **POUND BEEFSTEAK, IN ONE PIECE**

4 .... **CUPS VERY LIGHTLY SALTED WATER**

4 .... **ASIAN EGGPLANTS (2 POUNDS)**

1 .... **EGG, SEPARATED**

1 .... **TEASPOON CORN OIL**

3 .... **DRIED MUSHROOMS, SOAKED IN WATER FOR 1 HOUR, DRAINED AND CHOPPED**

4 OR 5 ... **HOT RED CHILI THREADS**

1 .... **TABLESPOON PINE NUTS**

1 .... **GARLIC CLOVE, CRUSHED**

3 .... **SCALLIONS, SLICED THIN**

⅛ ...... **TEASPOON BLACK PEPPER**

2 .... **TEASPOONS TOASTED SESAME SEEDS**

3 .... **TABLESPOONS SOY SAUCE MIXED WITH ½ CUP WATER**

1 Cut the beefsteak into halves. Chop 1 portion. Cut the other part into thin slices. Set aside.

2 Bring the 4 cups water to a boil in a large pan. Cut each eggplant into 3-inch crosswise pieces. Drop them into the water and cook over moderate heat for 3 minutes to soften. Drain and cool. Cut a 2-inch-deep incision into one end of each piece. Set aside.

3 Beat the egg white and yolk separately and lightly. Heat a small amount of oil in a skillet and fry a pancake of each part of the egg over low heat for about 1 minute. Cool and chop fine.

4 Mix the mushrooms, chili threads, pine nuts, garlic, scallions, pepper, sesame seeds and chopped egg pancakes together. Open each piece of eggplant and stuff with about 2 teaspoons of the stuffing.

5 Put the chopped and sliced beef on the bottom of a pan or in a large skillet. Add the soy sauce and water. Put the stuffed eggplant pieces on top, cover the pan, and simmer over moderate heat for 10 to 12 minutes.

Serve on a platter with the chopped and sliced beef on the bottom and the eggplant on top. Pour the sauce over all.

Serve warm.

Serves 6 with other dishes, including rice.

Kaji Jchim

STUFFED EGGPLANT II

Well-seasoned with fermented bean paste (*denjang*) and the hot chili paste (*gochu jang*) and cooked in its own liquid, the eggplants require little time to prepare, are fat-free and eminently tasty. They develop additional intensity of flavor when lightly reheated the next day.

2........	**LONG ASIAN EGGPLANTS, ABOUT 1 POUND**
¼	**POUND GROUND BEEF**
¼	**POUND GROUND PORK**
1........	**SEMI-HOT GREEN CHILI, SEEDED, SLICED THIN (⅓ CUP)**
1........	**MEDIUM-SIZE ONION, SLICED THIN (½ CUP)**
2 TO 3	**TABLESPOONS GOCHU JANG PASTE, TO TASTE**
1........	**TABLESPOON DENJANG PASTE**
1........	**TEASPOON KOREAN SESAME OIL**
½ TO 1....	**TEASPOON HOT RED CHILI POWDER**
½	**CUP WATER**

1 Trim off both ends of the eggplant, then cut into 3-inch-long pieces and stand on end. Make a crosscut 1 inch deep into one end of each piece. Set aside.

2 Prepare the stuffing. Mix together all the other ingredients except the water. Pry open the cut end of the eggplant pieces and pack in 2 tablespoons of the stuffing, smoothing it into a mound. Press together gently and place in 1 or 2 layers in a pan. Pour in the water, bring to a boil, cover the pan, and cook over low heat for 20 to 30 minutes. A spicy sauce will accumulate as the vegetables and water cook.

Serve warm with rice and salads.

Serves 4.

VARIATION: *All beef may be used instead of mixing beef and pork. The addition of pork, however, makes a softer and more flavorful stuffing.*

Beuseus Namul

STIR-FRIED DRIED MUSHROOMS

The best mushrooms are found in the mountainous area along the east coast of Korea. In this country with its ancient tradition of collecting and drying mushrooms, one can find many varieties, sizes and shapes in the public markets. After soaking, the very large mushrooms (I purchased some not less than 3 inches in diameter) take on the texture of a steak. How can the dedicated vegetarian beat that!

2 ...... **OUNCES DRIED MUSHROOMS, 6 TO 8**
1 ...... **TEASPOON KOREAN SESAME OIL**
1 ...... **TABLESPOON SOY SAUCE**
1 ...... **GARLIC CLOVE, CRUSHED**
¼ ...... **TEASPOON SUGAR**
⅛ ...... **TEASPOON PEPPER**
1 ...... **TEASPOON TOASTED SESAME SEEDS**

1 Soak the mushrooms in cold water for about 1 hour. Cold water will soften the mushrooms without extracting too much flavor. Drain and press them gently to eliminate excess liquid. Cut into ¼-inch-wide slices or tear them into quarters.

2 Heat the oil in a skillet and stir-fry the mushrooms over moderate heat for about 10 seconds, rapidly. Add the soy sauce, garlic, sugar and pepper and stir-fry continuously for ½ minute. Pour the mixture into a serving dish and garnish with the sesame seeds.

Serve as a side dish.

Serves 6 or more.

Beuseus Bockgee

DRIED MUSHROOM STIR-FRY

The season for fresh mushrooms is short in Korea and so the Koreans have, from ancient times, dried them to preserve them for the rest of the year and for export. Here is another version of the stir-fry.

20 ..... DRIED MUSHROOMS
3 ...... TABLESPOONS SOY SAUCE
2 ...... TABLESPOONS SUGAR
1 ...... TABLESPOON MINCED GARLIC
6 ...... SCALLIONS, CUT INTO 1-INCH PIECES
½ ..... POUND CHINESE CHIVES, CUT INTO ¼-INCH SLICES
1 ...... TEASPOON SESAME SEED SALT
¼ ..... TEASPOON BLACK PEPPER
1 ...... TABLESPOON KOREAN SESAME OIL
2 ...... TABLESPOONS CORN OIL

1 Rinse the mushrooms in cold water, then cover with fresh water and soak for 1 hour, or until soft. Cut each into 4 pieces; discard the stems.
2 Put everything except the corn oil into a bowl, mix well, and let stand for 15 minutes.
3 Heat the corn oil in a wok or large skillet, add all the ingredients, and stir-fry over moderate heat for 3 or 4 minutes to integrate all the seasonings.

Serve warm with rice and an assortment of side dishes of your choice.

Serves 4 to 6 with other dishes.

Pusud Muchim

FRESH MUSHROOM MIX

In Grandmother's House, a traditional restaurant in the city of Kwangju
where I spent several culinary days, the owner, a charming little old
lady wearing the knickers preferred by village women, presided over a
five-room restaurant. Just off the main street, one entered a narrow
alley with several unmarked doors. But which one was the restaurant?
A friend/translator and I, leaving our shoes outside, chose a plain
wooden door and entered a small courtyard seemingly only large
enough to turn around in, but with an atmosphere of tranquility. As in
all of the traditional Korean restaurants there is no bustle of clients
waiting to be seated in one of the small rooms.

The food was home-cooked regional fare served all together on
the low dining tables. The service featured 27 different dishes, each
one serving two, including the inevitable but welcome bowl of glutinous rice spotted with black beans. Most dishes were designed to
enhance the appetite—such as the salted baby shrimps, a small dish of
pickled oyster stomachs, chili-hot kimchi, crisp and chewy sweet and
sour tiny anchovies, a yellow bean-paste soup with zucchini and this
Mushroom Mix among others. All this for $3.50 per person!

1/4...... **POUND FRESH, LARGE, MEATY SHIITAKE
MUSHROOMS, CAPS ONLY**

1 ...... **TEASPOON CORN OIL**

1/4...... **TEASPOON SALT**

1 ...... **GARLIC CLOVE, CRUSHED**

1 ...... **TEASPOON THIN-SLICED FRESH
HOT GREEN CHILI**

1/2...... **TEASPOON KOREAN SESAME OIL**

1 Rinse the mushroom caps well and cut them into 1/4-inch-wide slices.
2 Heat the corn oil in a skillet, add the mushrooms and salt, and stir-
fry over moderate heat for 2 minutes. Add the garlic and chili and continue to fry for 2 minutes more. Stir in the sesame oil and remove from
the heat. Cool to room temperature.

Serve as a side dish with other Korean foods and rice.

Serves 2 or 3.

NOTE: *The chili is rinsed in cold water to remove the seeds. This is not only for
aesthetic reasons but also serves to dilute the intensity of the chili.*

Goguma Chilge Muchim

The sweet potato vine with its mass of leaves is popular in Korea but only as a side dish. The young vines are stripped of their leaves and stir-fried with or without mushrooms to provide one side dish that mercifully does not contain hot chili and is therefore a contrast to the other dishes.

1 ...... TABLESPOON CORN OIL

¼ ..... POUND SWEET POTATO VINE, CUT INTO 3-INCH LENGTHS

¼ ..... POUND FRESH MEATY MUSHROOMS, CAPS ONLY, SLICED

1 ...... GARLIC CLOVE, CRUSHED

1 ...... SMALL CARROT, CUT INTO JULIENNE STRIPS (⅓ CUP)

1 ...... TEASPOON SALT, OR TO TASTE

1 ...... TEASPOON KOREAN SESAME OIL

Heat the oil in a wok or skillet. Add the vine and mushrooms and stir-fry over moderate heat for 1 minute. Add all the other ingredients and stir-fry for 8 to 10 minutes.

Serve warm or at room temperature.

Serves 4.

VARIATION: Hobak Muchim—Zucchini and Mushroom Stir-Fry
Substitute 1 small zucchini, sliced ⅛-inch thick (1 cup) for the sweet potato vine. Follow the same method and timing.

Da Shima Twigim

The hallmark of Korean cooking is the use of natural foods in appealing ways. Seaweed, which is now domesticated, that is to say raised on farms jutting out into the sea, supplements food that is raised on land. Containing iodine and a host of other minerals and with a flavor reminiscent of an ocean breeze, the fried kelp (*Laminaria japonica*) with a light sprinkling of sugar is an example of the culinary ingenuity of the Koreans.

- **10 ..... PIECES, 3-INCH SIZE, OF DRIED BLACK KELP**
- **1 ...... CUP CORN OIL**
- **2 ...... TABLESPOONS SUGAR**

1 Wipe each piece of the dried kelp with a damp (not soaking) cloth.
2 Heat the oil in a skillet over moderate heat. One at a time, put a very lightly dampened piece of kelp in the hot oil, holding it with chopsticks, until the color changes to dark green. Bubbles may appear on the kelp surface and it will develop a crispness.
3 While the kelp is still hot sprinkle on a few grains of sugar. The sugar will cling to the kelp when it is still hot and just removed from the oil. It will not do so when cold.

Eat as a side dish or snack food with tea or a drink.

Serves 4 to 6.

Gim Gui

The dried black seaweed (laver) is usually purchased in paper-thin sheets about 6 x 8 inches, and this was the size I found in the open market in Pusan harbor. After roasting and before serving, they are cut into rectangles 2½ x 3½ inches. In times past, when open wood fires were the method of cooking, the Korean housewife, so I've been told, would hold each sheet with chopsticks and wave it back and forth over the heat without getting too close to the flame. This would toast the seasoned sheets, which turn a dark brown with a touch of green. Now we toast the sheets in a skillet.

20........... DRIED BLACK LAVER SEAWEED SHEETS
KOREAN SESAME OIL
SALT

1 Smear each sheet with a few drops of oil and with the back of a spoon spread it over the surface on one side. The sheets are fragile and the touch should be light. Sprinkle each sheet with a few grains of salt.
2 Heat a large skillet or nonstick pan over low heat for 1 minute. When the skillet is hot, press the oiled laver into the pan for a brief time, which will turn the color into a brownish dark green, indicating the sheet is toasted. Remove it quickly.
3 Now cut each sheet down the middle lengthwise. Cut each half across so that there are 4 small sheets. Put all the small, oiled, toasted sheets one on top of the other in a pile. Plunge a sturdy toothpick into the center of the pile, which will hold all of them together.

Serve the laver with rice. The seaweed can also be eaten out of hand as a snack with drinks, or sliced into strips and used as a garnish for soups or other foods.

Kye Ran Kim Maroom

These tidy and attractive rolls are bite-size finger food with golden egg and black laver layers. Easy to prepare and ideal for cocktail parties or to accompany a glass of wine at home, the rolls are made in a square frying pan in Asian kitchens. Nevertheless, a round skillet or griddle will do the job.

3 ...... EGGS
¼ ...... TEASPOON SALT
2 OR 3 ... TABLESPOONS CORN OIL FOR PANFRYING
SEVERAL SHEETS OF DRIED BLACK LAVER

1 Beat the eggs and salt together. Heat 2 teaspoons oil in a square pan over low heat and tilt it around so that the bottom is covered. Put just enough beaten egg in the pan to cover the bottom when the pan is quickly tilted. Fry for a few seconds, remove the pan from the heat, and while the egg is slightly moist lay 1 sheet of the dried seaweed over it.

2 Now loosen the egg/seaweed cake from the pan and roll it away from yourself to the other side of the pan. Push the roll to the center of the pan and brown it lightly over low heat for 1 minute. Repeat, to use up the eggs.

Cool the rolls (they do not cut well when hot) and cut into 1-inch-wide slices.

Serve at room temperature with tea or drinks.

Makes 8 rolls.

Tubu Sang Che

CRUSHED BEAN-CURD SALAD

Bean curd is known as *tofu* in Japan and China, *tahu* in Indonesia and *tubu* in Korea. It is a high-protein food universally appreciated in most of Asia, except India. It is eclectic and can be eaten raw, boiled or crisply fried. The following salad is Korean in concept and has been enriched with the crunchy texture of Korean radish. The soft bean curd with its creamy texture (sometimes called Japanese-style) is used here.

¼ ..... **POUND KOREAN RADISH, PEELED, CUT INTO 2-INCH-LONG JULIENNE STRIPS**

1 ...... **TEASPOON SALT**

2 ...... **SQUARES OF SOFT BEAN CURD**

1 ...... **GARLIC CLOVE, CRUSHED**

2 ...... **TEASPOONS KOREAN SESAME OIL**

2 ...... **TEASPOONS SOY SAUCE**

1 TO 2 ... **TEASPOONS HOT RED CHILI POWDER, TO TASTE**

1 Mix the radish and salt together and let stand for ½ hour. Then gently squeeze out the accumulated liquid in a towel.

2 Dry the bean curd on a towel and mash with a fork not too smoothly. Mix this with the radish and stir in the garlic, sesame oil, soy sauce and chili powder.

Refrigerate and serve cold as a side dish with other foods.

Serves 4.

Sookju Namul

BEAN-SPROUT SALAD WITH SESAME

Namul is the word used for vegetable dishes and in this case it refers to
bean sprouts. Simple in execution and seasoned with standard
ingredients in which the sesame seeds and oil are paramount, the
salad is a healthy adjunct to any main course whether it be of the East
or the West.

1/2	**POUND FRESH BEAN SPROUTS**
3	**CUPS BOILING WATER**
1	**TEASPOON SALT**
1	**SCALLION, SLICED, WHITE PART HALVED LENGTHWISE**
1	**GARLIC CLOVE, CRUSHED OR CHOPPED FINE**
1/8	**TEASPOON PEPPER**
1/2	**TEASPOON KOREAN SESAME OIL**
1	**TEASPOON TOASTED SESAME SEEDS OR BLACK SESAME SEEDS**

1 Put the bean sprouts into the boiling water with 1/2 teaspoon salt.
Cover and cook for 1 minute. Remove pan from the heat, still covered,
and let stand and steam for 2 minutes more. Drain well and with your
hands press out the excess liquid firmly.
2 Put the sprouts into a serving bowl, add all the other ingredients
including remaining 1/2 teaspoon salt, and mix and toss. Adjust the salt
if necessary and serve at room temperature.

Serves 4 with other dishes.

NOTE: *Sesame seeds can be purchased toasted but it is suggested that they be toasted
in a dry nonstick skillet for 2 or 3 minutes more to emphasize the sesame flavor.*

Oee Namul Muchim

CUCUMBER SALAD

This is an ideal salad to serve as a side dish with traditional Korean foods. Remember that hot chili should be used to taste, yet by diluting the chili too much its special impact is lost and the salad is so modified that it becomes trivial. Koreans have a higher degree of heat tolerance than we do and to enjoy Korean food to its fullest, one must develop a taste for the chili.

I learned to make this salad from a Korean cook who had a very heavy hand with the chili powder. During one of my gasping sessions, she would say to me rather slyly, "Shall I call the fire department?"

3 ...... **KIRBY CUCUMBERS**
2 ...... **SCALLIONS, SLICED THIN**
1 ...... **TEASPOON KOREAN SESAME OIL**
2 ...... **TEASPOONS CIDER VINEGAR**
1 ...... **TEASPOON HOT RED CHILI POWDER, OR TO TASTE**
½ ..... **TEASPOON SALT**
½ ..... **TEASPOON SUGAR**

1 Trim both ends of the cucumbers and cut off 2 narrow strips of skin from each to produce a design. Slice the cucumbers thin, diagonally.
2 Mix all the ingredients together and toss the salad well.

Serve cold or at room temperature.

Serves 4.

Kaji Namul

Small plates of a variety of steamed but cold salads are invariably served with Korean food—one of the standard features of their dining style at home and in restaurants. This eggplant salad is an example of a fat-free, vegetarian side dish relevant for these times of less meat and more vegetables.

1 ...... **ASIAN EGGPLANT, 1/2 POUND**
2 ...... **SCALLIONS, CHOPPED**
1/2 ..... **TEASPOON SALT**
1 ...... **TEASPOON SOY SAUCE**
1/8 ..... **TEASPOON PEPPER**
1/2 ..... **TEASPOON TOASTED SESAME SEEDS**
1/2 ..... **TEASPOON KOREAN SESAME OIL**

1 Trim about 1/2 inch from each end of the eggplant. Then place it in a Chinese-style steamer and steam over hot water until tender, for 10 to 12 minutes. Cool the eggplant and tear into 3-inch-long strips.
2 Toss the eggplant together with all the other ingredients. Refrigerate until ready to serve but serve at room temperature.

Serves 2.

Kaji Namul

EGGPLANT SALAD WITH RED CHILI

Asian eggplants are long and slender with deep purple skins and very few seeds, unlike the western bulbous eggplants which do have many seeds and much water. The Kaji Namul is a side dish served with an assortment of foods in the Korean manner but could quite easily become a salad for western tables if prepared in larger quantities.

3 .... ASIAN EGGPLANTS, 1½ POUNDS, ENDS TRIMMED

1 .... SCALLION, SLICED

4 .... GARLIC CLOVES, SLICED THIN

1 TO 3 .... TEASPOONS FRESH HOT RED CHILI, SLICED VERY THIN, TO TASTE

2 .... TABLESPOONS SOY SAUCE

1 .... TABLESPOON TOASTED SESAME SEEDS MIXED WITH 1 TEASPOON SALT

1 .... TABLESPOON KOREAN SESAME OIL

2 .... TEASPOONS WHITE OR CIDER VINEGAR

1 Cut the eggplants lengthwise into halves. Steam them in a Chinese-style steamer until soft, about 15 minutes. Cool and tear them into long thin strips.

2 Crush the scallion and garlic into a paste. Rinse the chili in cold water to remove the seeds, and drain.

3 Put the scallion, garlic, chili, soy sauce, sesame seeds, oil and vinegar into a bowl and mix well. Add the eggplant strips and toss everything together.

Serve cold as a side dish with other Korean foods or alone with rice for the dedicated vegetarian.

Serves 4.

Sangchussam

Serving these lettuce sandwiches is a popular and tasty method of utilizing the long, green lettuce leaves while fulfilling the Korean principle that food should be attractive, healthful, fresh and delicious. They can be a simple leaf with a slather of seasoning paste or a more elaborate one with additional filler. In any event, texture and flavor are predominant characteristics. Use loose-leaved types of lettuce such as the red or green leaf, Boston or Romaine kinds that are flexible and can be folded into a neat packet. It would not be unthinkable for a person to eat 4 or 5 sandwiches to accompany other traditional Korean foods. Select leaves that are fresh and unblemished.

12 TO 16.... LETTUCE LEAVES OF YOUR CHOICE

Seasoning Paste

2........TABLESPOONS DENJANG

1........TABLESPOON GOCHU JANG

2........GARLIC CLOVES, SLICED THIN

¼.......TEASPOON TOASTED SESAME SEEDS

¼.......TEASPOON KOREAN SESAME OIL

Fillings

THIN SLICES OF EGG WHITE AND EGG YOLK OMELETS

JULIENNE SLIVERS OF KIRBY CUCUMBER SKIN

JULIENNE SLIVERS OF SEMI-HOT, SEEDED GREEN CHILI

DRIED MUSHROOMS, SOAKED IN WATER FOR 1 HOUR, DRAINED, SLICED THIN

DRIED TREE EARS, SOAKED IN WATER FOR 1 HOUR, DRAINED, SLICED THIN

1 Rinse the lettuce in cold water, drain and dry.

2 Prepare the seasoning paste. Mix together the denjang, gochu jang, garlic, sesame seeds and oil. Set aside.

3 Prepare as many fillings as you wish.

4 Take 1 leaf of lettuce and spread over it 1 teaspoon of the seasoning paste. Then add as many optional ingredients as you wish or none at all, as I often do. Fold the leaf over 2 or 3 times into a round roll and eat as many as wanted to accompany traditional Korean foods.

Serve at room temperature.

Serves 4.

Sangchu Kutjuri

MIXED SIMPLE SALAD

Koreans like the red leaf lettuce with its curled edges, tender texture and variegated color. Torn rather than cut into 2- or 3-inch pieces, the lettuce still retains its natural configuration.

6 TO 8 ... LARGE LETTUCE LEAVES, TORN INTO PIECES (RED LEAF LETTUCE PREFERRED)

2 ...... SCALLIONS, CUT INTO 1-INCH PIECES, WHITE PART ONLY IS SPLIT LENGTHWISE

2 ...... TEASPOONS CIDER VINEGAR

1 ...... TABLESPOON SOY SAUCE

¼ ...... TEASPOON SUGAR

2 ...... TEASPOONS KOREAN SESAME OIL

½ TO 1 ... TEASPOON HOT RED CHILI POWDER, TO TASTE

Put the lettuce into a salad bowl; scatter the scallion pieces over the top. Add all the other ingredients, then toss the salad.

Serve cold or at room temperature.

Serves 4.

‡ **NOTE:** *Boston or any other kind of loose-leaf lettuce may be used instead of the red leaf.*

Sang Meenari Muchim

Crisp, attractively bitter stems of watercress (*Nasturtium officinale*) are
combined with Korean seasonings to prepare a salad for all seasons.
Watercress is high in vitamins A and C as well as minerals. Note that the
chili powder is to taste and more or less may be added to your own
degree of tolerance.

- 1 ...... **BUNCH OF FRESH WATERCRESS, THICK ENDS TRIMMED OFF AND SPRIGS CUT INTO HALVES**
- 1 ...... **TABLESPOON CIDER VINEGAR**
- 2 ...... **TABLESPOONS SOY SAUCE**
- 1 ...... **TEASPOON SESAME SALT**
- ¼ ..... **TEASPOON SUGAR**
- ¼ ..... **TEASPOON KOREAN SESAME OIL**
- ½ ..... **TEASPOON HOT RED CHILI POWDER**

Mix everything together and toss well.

Serve cold or at room temperature.

Serves 4.

VARIATION: *For those diners who prefer a less peppery flavor and a different texture, there is a cooked version. Cook the watercress in 3 cups water for 1 minute, rinse under cold water, and press firmly to eliminate all liquid. Omit the sugar and chili powder but add a crushed garlic clove and 2 sliced scallions, and proceed as in the basic recipe*

Oyee Beturi

CUCUMBER AND BEEF SEASONED SALAD

Slender young cucumbers are used in Korean food as garnishes, in hot soups as well as in cold dishes. They are never peeled. They add texture and flavor wherever used. I well remember the hot day in August when I tasted this unconventional and attractive Korean salad in the city of Kyongju, the ancient capital of the Silla Kingdom.

Seasoning

1 ...... TABLESPOON SOY SAUCE

1 ...... TEASPOON SUGAR

1 ...... SCALLION, WHITE PART ONLY, CRUSHED TO A PASTE

1 ...... GARLIC CLOVE, CRUSHED TO A PASTE

2 ...... TEASPOONS TOASTED SESAME SEEDS MIXED WITH 1/2 TEASPOON SALT

1/4 ...... TEASPOON BLACK PEPPER

1 ...... TEASPOON KOREAN SESAME OIL

Salad

3 ...... YOUNG CUCUMBERS, ABOUT 1/2 POUND, NOT PEELED

SALTWATER BRINE OF 2 CUPS WATER AND 2 TEASPOONS SALT

2 ...... DRIED MUSHROOMS, SOAKED IN WATER FOR 1 HOUR, DRAINED, SLICED THIN

1/4 ...... POUND STEAK, CUT INTO THIN 2-INCH-LONG SLICES

2 ...... TEASPOONS CORN OIL

10 ..... DRIED RED CHILI THREADS, CUT INTO 2-INCH LENGTHS

1 Mix seasoning ingredients together and set aside.

2 Cut the cucumbers in a domino shape 2 inches long, 1/4 inch thick and 1 inch wide. Soak in the brine for 10 minutes. Drain and press out the excess liquid in a towel.

3 Toss the mushrooms and beef with the seasoning mixture and stir-fry in 1 teaspoon oil over moderate heat for 2 minutes. Cool. Separately, stir-fry the cucumbers in 1 teaspoon oil for 1 minute. Cool.

4 Now toss the beef, cucumbers and chili threads together until well mixed. Refrigerate.

Serve cold or at room temperature.

Serves 4 as a side dish.

Soegan Kong Pat Nenche

COLD BEEF LIVER AND KIDNEY SALAD

This large cold salad, made with such unconventional salad ingredients
as liver and kidney, is attractively arranged on a platter and served
with a powerful seasoning dip. The Soegan Kong is a popular dish
for any party held during the hot days of summer—whether a wedding celebration, a birthday party or a special holiday.

Note the amount of fresh ginger used—shredded in cooking the
meat, in julienne strips on the platter and chopped in the dip.

1 ...... **POUND VEAL OR BEEF LIVER, IN ONE PIECE**

1 ...... **POUND VEAL OR BEEF KIDNEY, WHOLE**

2 ...... **TABLESPOONS SALT**

2 ...... **TABLESPOONS SHREDDED FRESH GINGER**

5 ...... **SCALLIONS, CUT INTO 2-INCH LENGTHS, SHREDDED, SOAKED IN COLD WATER FOR 10 MINUTES, WELL DRAINED**

2 ...... **KIRBY CUCUMBERS, CUT INTO 2-INCH LENGTHS, ¾ INCH WIDE, ⅛ INCH THICK**

¼ ..... **POUND FRESH GINGER, PEELED AND CUT INTO 2-INCH-LONG JULIENNE SLIVERS**

Dip

¾ ..... **CUP SOY SAUCE**

2 ...... **TABLESPOONS CHOPPED SCALLION**

1 ...... **TABLESPOON CHOPPED GINGER**

2 ...... **TABLESPOONS SUGAR**

3 ...... **TABLESPOONS CIDER OR WHITE VINEGAR**

1 ...... **TABLESPOON KOREAN SESAME OIL**

1 Place the liver and kidney in separate pans, cover with water, divide
the salt and shredded ginger between them, and cook over moderate
heat for 20 minutes. Drain well, and cool. Slice the meats into 2-inch-
long pieces, ⅛ inch thick. Set aside.

(Continued next page)

2 Use a platter large enough to contain all the meats and vegetables and cover it with shredded scallions. Arrange the liver and kidney, alternating and overlapping, with a strip of cucumber between the meats in a border around the edge of the platter. Next make an inner circle with a 2-inch-wide band of the julienned ginger. Save the center of the platter for the seasoning dip.

3 Mix the dip ingredients together and pour into one bowl for the center of the platter, or present the dip in individual small sauce dishes to each diner. Serve at room temperature with other appropriate dishes.

Serves 8 to 10 as a side dish.

Nagchi Sengchi

When sliced vegetables are salted they release their liquid, which can
then be squeezed out. This gives a salad more concentrated flavor
and a somewhat different texture. Combined with octopus slices and
a vivid Korean-style sauce, the salad then becomes an important dish
on its own rather than being just an adjunct to a meal.

1 ½..... **CUPS 2-INCH DIAGONAL SLICES OF HEARTS OF CELERY WITH A FEW TENDER LEAVES**

2 ...... **SCALLIONS, GREEN PART ONLY, CUT INTO 3-INCH-LONG JULIENNE SLIVERS**

1 ...... **MEDIUM-SIZE CARROT, CUT INTO 2-INCH-LONG JULIENNE SLIVERS (1 CUP)**

1 ...... **CUP FRESH CHRYSANTHEMUM LEAVES, CUT INTO 3-INCH-LONG PIECES**

1 ...... **KIRBY CUCUMBER, CUT INTO 2-INCH-LONG JULIENNE SLIVERS**

1 ...... **CUP 2-INCH-LONG JULIENNE SLIVERS OF KOREAN RADISH, PEELED**

2 ...... **CUPS SHREDDED CHINESE CABBAGE (OPTIONAL)**

COARSE SALT

½ ..... **POUND COOKED OCTOPUS, CUT INTO THIN 2-INCH SLICES**

½ ..... **RECIPE OF NAGCHI BOEKUM SAUCE (SEE P. 191) IN WHICH YOU HAVE MIXED 2 TABLESPOONS CIDER VINEGAR**

1 Select 5 of the vegetables you wish to use and sprinkle them separately with 1 teaspoon salt each. Toss and let stand for 10 minutes.
Then rinse under cold water and squeeze out quite firmly. Set each
vegetable aside.

2 Mix the vegetables, octopus and sauce together. Toss well and
refrigerate. The salad can be served immediately or the next day
when the flavor is more intense.

Serve cold or at room temperature.

Serves 6 with other dishes.

Ojingau Kyouja Seng Chie

SEAFOOD SALAD IN MUSTARD SAUCE

The mustard is pungent, the vegetables are colorful, and the seafood, lightly blanched in boiling water, retains all its ocean flavor. The salad is eaten with white rice and is a complete Korean meal with all its culinary characteristics intact.

Seafood

3 ...... LARGE SQUID, ABOUT 1½ POUNDS

¼ ..... POUND MEDIUM SHRIMPS, PEELED, DEVEINED AND HALVED LENGTHWISE

1 ...... KIRBY CUCUMBER, CUT INTO VERY THIN SLICES ½ INCH WIDE, 3 INCHES LONG

1 ...... SMALL CARROT, CUT THE SAME SIZE AS THE CUCUMBER

1 ...... GREEN PEPPER, SEEDED, CUT THE SAME SIZE AS THE CUCUMBER

Sauce

3 ...... TABLESPOONS DRY MUSTARD

3 ...... TABLESPOONS SUGAR

3 ...... TABLESPOONS WHITE OR CIDER VINEGAR

3 ...... TABLESPOONS BOILING WATER

1 ...... TEASPOON SALT

1 ...... TABLESPOON PINE NUTS, CRUSHED WITH THE FLAT OF A KNIFE, FOR GARNISH

1 Clean the squid in conventional fashion. Cut the body into pieces ½ inch wide and 3 inches long. Cut the tentacles 3 inches long. Bring a pan half filled with water to a rapid boil. Put the squid pieces and shrimps in a strainer and plunge it into the water for 5 seconds. This is just enough to cook them very slightly. Drain and cool. Prepare the vegetables and set aside.

2 To prepare the sauce, mix the mustard, sugar, vinegar, boiling water and salt together smoothly.

3 When ready to serve the salad and only at this time, mix the vegetables and seafood together and add mustard sauce according to taste. Toss well and garnish the salad with the pine nuts.

Serve cold or at room temperature with plain white rice and an assortment of side dishes.

Serves 6.

NOTE: *There are those Koreans who prepare seafood salad made with raw seafood. Slice and rinse the squid, peel and devein the shrimps and toss with the vegetables and mustard sauce. This should only be done by people who live near pristine waters and have complete confidence in its cleanliness.*

There are others who prefer seafood rapidly cooked for 1 minute (I am one of those), drained, cooled and tossed with the vegetables and mustard sauce. This timing is not enough to toughen the squid.

The standard recipe simply blanches the seafood in boiling water for a few seconds, as this recipe indicates.

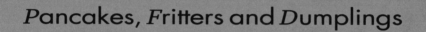

Pancakes, Fritters and Dumplings

My introduction to Pa Jon, the very popular scallion pancake, was at a small, neat restaurant around the corner from my hotel in Seoul. The chef was preparing a Korean pancake on a good-size, lightly oiled griddle placed in the window facing a busy street. First a seasoned batter was poured in the customary rectangular shape onto a grill warming up over low heat. Then lengths of scallions were placed over and into the batter and a few fresh oysters and clams were pushed into the surface here and there. Several very thin slices of fresh hot green chili were scattered over all. A tablespoon or two of batter was sprinkled over the surface to hold the vegetables and seafood in place. All this took 3 minutes—just long enough to make the pancake firm. It was turned over and the second side was cooked just long enough for the pancake to set and for the ingredients to be cooked.

This procedure for large or small pancakes was repeated innumerable times for me all over Korea and became the standard by which I was able to observe the correct technique of making a Pa Jon.

Koreans enjoy the large variety of pancakes and fritters that they can prepare at home or buy as street food. They can be vegetarian or made with meat and seafood, round or square, thick or thin. They can be eaten warm off the griddle or at room temperature. On a picnic near the West Sea, I devoured several Bindaedok and they were cold.

One only needs to choreograph the combinations and the event, prepare the batter, add anything you want in the way of vegetables, meat or seafood, and fry lightly on a griddle or large skillet. They may or may not be eaten with a dip but are better, in my opinion, with a well-seasoned dip.

Batters are prepared with wheat flour, glutinous rice, or buckwheat flour, which I encountered frequently on the island of Cheju. Water is the principal liquid used to make the batter although occasionally an egg is beaten in. The heat element is kept low so that there is ample time to add ingredients to the surface of the pancake. The object is to cook the pancake slowly until the ingredients have softened and the pancake is a light beige—not dark brown. Aesthetics are important.

Their fritters are more like ours. Vegetables, seafood and meat are dipped into flour and egg and fried briefly until crisp. They can be appetizers in the western sense or side dishes on the Korean table; the borders are blurred. If the cook is good the food is good and the definitions are irrelevant.

Pa Jon

This is a version of a scallion pancake, such a popular Korean snack/entrée that it invites variations from one family to another. In this case, besides the small nugget of ground beef, carrot and sweet peppers are added to the batter to provide additional flavor.

1 ...... CUP FLOUR

1 ...... TEASPOON SALT

1½ ..... CUPS COLD WATER OR ENOUGH TO ENSURE A MODERATELY THIN BATTER

3 ...... OUNCES GROUND BEEF

4 ...... SCALLIONS, ROOT ENDS TRIMMED, CUT INTO 2-INCH LENGTHS

2 ...... OUNCES SWEET RED AND/OR GREEN PEPPER, CUT INTO 2-INCH JULIENNE STRIPS

CORN OIL FOR PANFRYING

1 Mix together the flour, salt, water and beef. Add the scallions and peppers and mix thoroughly but gently.

2 Heat an 8-inch skillet. Add the oil for panfrying and warm up over moderate heat. Then add half the batter mixture which should make a pancake about ¼ inch thick, and fry it on both sides for 3 or 4 minutes. Slip the pancake onto a cutting board and cut into 3-inch pieces. Then quickly reassemble the pieces into their original pancake shape. (Or you may present the uncut pancake, which is then divided at the table.)

Serve warm with a traditional dip made of 2 tablespoons soy sauce, ¼ teaspoon Korean sesame oil, ½ teaspoon toasted sesame seeds, 1 teaspoon thin-sliced scallion and ½ teaspoon dried hot red chili flakes.

Makes 2 pancakes.

Pa Jon

CLASSICAL KOREAN PANCAKES

These same pancakes in their simplest form—just batter and a handful of scallions—are prepared by street vendors and sell for a few pennies. The recipe given here is more complex, with a variety of ingredients, and is more apt to be served in a restaurant. It comes from the city of Kyongju, and is just one of the many versions prevalent throughout the country.

Note that the addition of rice or rice flour produces a chewy texture and crisp edges.

1 ...... **CUP GLUTINOUS RICE**

2 ...... **CUPS FLOUR**

2 ...... **CUPS WATER**

2 ...... **EGGS, BEATEN**

1/4 ...... **TEASPOON SALT**

8 ...... **SPRIGS OF CHINESE CHIVES, CUT INTO 3-INCH PIECES (OPTIONAL)**

6 ...... **SCALLIONS, GREEN PART ONLY, CUT INTO JULIENNE STRIPS 3 INCHES LONG**

2 ...... **TABLESPOONS FINE-CHOPPED BEEFSTEAK**

6 ...... **MUSSELS, REMOVED FROM SHELL**

6 ...... **FRESH OYSTERS OR CLAMS, REMOVED FROM SHELL**

CORN OIL FOR PANFRYING

1 Soak the rice in water to cover for 3 hours. Drain and process to a paste.

2 Mix the flour, rice paste, water, eggs, salt, chives, scallions, beef, mussels, oysters or clams together. Heat the oil in a skillet and add about 1 cup of the mixture in a rectangular shape 4 by 5 inches. Brown over low heat for 2 minutes, turn the pancake over with a spatula, and lightly brown for 2 or 3 minutes more. The pancake should not be fried to a dark brown but lightly cooked over low heat to a beige or tan color.

Prepare all the pancakes this way.

Serve warm, cut into 8 pieces for easy handling.

Makes 6 pancakes.

Tongurangteng

MINIATURE MEAT PANCAKES

The island of Cheju, south of the Korean peninsula, which I circumambulated
several times over several days, has a number of specialties not found
on the mainland. This miniature version of the pancake, combining
the batter with vegetables and just a taste of meat, is one of them.

1 ...... **CUP FLOUR**
1 ...... **EGG, BEATEN**
1/2 ..... **CUP WATER, ABOUT**
1/4 ..... **TEASPOON SALT**
1/8 ..... **TEASPOON BLACK PEPPER**
2 ...... **SCALLIONS, GREEN PART ONLY,
CHOPPED FINE**
3 ...... **TABLESPOONS FINE-CHOPPED
(NOT GROUND) PORK OR BEEFSTEAK**
2 ...... **TABLESPOONS GRATED CARROT**
3 ...... **TABLESPOONS CORN OIL FOR PANFRYING**

1 Mix everything together except the oil, using only enough water to
prepare a thick batter.
2 Heat the oil in a skillet and drop in a heaping tablespoon of the batter.
Press down to shape a pancake that is about 2 inches in diameter. Lightly
brown over moderate heat for 3 minutes on each side.

Serve warm with a soy sauce dip of your choice.

Makes 8 pancakes.

Cheju-do Bindaedoek

RADISH-STUFFED BUCKWHEAT PANCAKE

A traditional specialty of the island of Cheju is prepared with buckwheat flour—an unconventional grain for Asia, one that is usually associated with Eastern Europe. Noodles are also made with buckwheat flour on the Korean mainland, where they are included in soups.

- 1 ...... **CUP JULIENNE STRIPS OF KOREAN RADISH**
- ½ ..... **TEASPOON SALT**
- ½ ..... **TEASPOON SUGAR**
- 1 ...... **TEASPOON TOASTED SESAME SEEDS**
- 2 ...... **SCALLIONS, CUT INTO JULIENNE STRIPS 2 INCHES LONG**
- 4 ...... **CUPS BUCKWHEAT FLOUR**
- 2 ...... **CUPS WATER**
- **CORN OIL FOR PAN OR GRIDDLE FRYING**

1 Toss together the radish, salt, sugar, sesame seeds and scallions. Set aside for 15 minutes.

2 Make a relatively thin batter with the flour and enough water to reach the desired consistency. Oil an 8-inch skillet with about 2 teaspoons oil and heat over low flame. Pour ¾ cup of the batter into the pan and tilt so batter will cover bottom. Fry over low heat for 3 minutes to set the batter and lightly brown the bottom. Remove the pancake to a plate. Prepare all the batter this way.

3 Put 2 heaping tablespoons of the radish mix on the end of the pancake nearest you and roll it over twice. Fill remaining pancakes in the same way.

Serve warm or at room temperature, with or without your favorite dip.

Makes 6 pancakes.

Gool Pa Jon

The generic name of these pancakes is *jon*, one of the most popular of all Korean snacks. When preceded by *pa*, it indicates a scallion pancake; *gool* is oyster, *buchu* is Chinese chives and *hobak* is zucchini. All of them are quickly prepared for unexpected guests, family gatherings or for any occasion. Koreans dote on *jon*.

On farms in the Korean countryside, the women prepare large quantities of the Pa Jon since bunches of mammoth scallions, some of which are from 20 to 30 inches long, are so readily available. Individual pancakes, not more than ¼ inch thick, cooked with a layer of scallions on top, take time to prepare but are very attractive to serve. You will save time by preparing one large pancake 10 to 12 inches across, or the largest your skillet will accommodate, and then cutting it into manageable pieces. This is the way it is usually handled in restaurants. The farmer's wine, mukhuli, is so compatible with the Pa Jon that one usually orders them together for a snack.

Note that the glutinous rice flour produces a chewy texture as well as a crispness around the edge of the pancake.

Jon Batter

1	**CUP FLOUR**
1	**CUP WATER**
¼	**CUP GLUTINOUS RICE FLOUR**
1	**EGG, BEATEN**
½	**TEASPOON SALT**

Mix all the ingredients together, rubbing out any lumps of flour to make a smooth batter. Use this batter for all types of pancakes.

Makes 2 cups.

½	**CUP FRESH OYSTERS**
1	**TEASPOON SALT**
	CORN OIL FOR PANFRYING
1	**TEASPOON SESAME SALT**
2	**SCALLIONS WITH THIN STALKS**
1	**CUP STANDARD JON BATTER**

1 Mix the oysters and salt together, then rinse under cold water and drain. Heat 1 teaspoon oil in a skillet, add the sesame salt, and stir-fry the oysters lightly for ½ minute. Set aside.

(Continued next page)

2 Cut the green leaves of the scallions into 3-inch pieces. Slice the white part lengthwise into 4 pieces, each 3 inches long. Set aside.
3 Mix the scallions and batter together. Heat about 1 tablespoon oil in a skillet over low heat. Scoop in 2 heaping tablespoons of the batter, forming a rectangular shape the length of the scallion. Press into it 1 or 2 oysters and fry the pancake on one side for 2 minutes. Turn it over and very lightly brown it on the other side. The color should remain golden rather than dark brown, with a few flecks of darker color. Drain the pancakes on paper towels.

Serve warm with or without a dip.

Makes 4 or 5 pancakes.

VARIATION: *If you omit the oysters but otherwise make the recipe as given, you will have a Scallion Pancake or Pa Jon.*
OTHER VARIATIONS: *Buchu Jon (Chinese Chive Pancake): Omit the scallions and add 8 Chinese chives cut into 3-inch lengths and 1 small onion sliced thin. Mix into batter and proceed as in other recipes. Hobak Jon (Zucchini Pancake): Add 1 cup very thin zucchini slices and 1/3 cup thin onion slices to 1 cup batter and proceed as before.*

Jon Dip I

3	TABLESPOONS SOY SAUCE
1	TEASPOON CHOPPED GARLIC
1	TABLESPOON CHOPPED SCALLION, GREEN PART ONLY
1/4	TEASPOON BLACK PEPPER
1	TABLESPOON TOASTED SESAME SEEDS
1	TEASPOON KOREAN SESAME OIL
1	TEASPOON CIDER VINEGAR

Mix everything together briskly and use with any pancakes, but especially with Oyster Pancakes.

Nogdoo Bindaedoek

Mung beans are the beans that several Asian cultures use to produce bean sprouts. The skinless mung beans are yellow and it is possible to purchase them skinned in Korean groceries and supermarkets.

Batter

1 ...... **POUND YELLOW SKINLESS MUNG BEANS (SEE NOTE)**
1/2 ...... **POUND BEAN SPROUTS**
1 ...... **CUP CABBAGE PICKLE (SEE P. 28-29)**
3 ...... **EGGS, BEATEN**
1/4 ...... **CUP FLOUR**
1/2 ...... **POUND TENDER BEEF OR PORK STEAK, CUT INTO JULIENNE SLIVERS**
2 ...... **GARLIC CLOVES, CHOPPED FINE**
1 ...... **TABLESPOON CHOPPED SCALLION**
1 ...... **TEASPOON SALT**
1/4 ...... **TEASPOON PEPPER**
1 ...... **TABLESPOON KOREAN SESAME OIL**
1 ...... **TABLESPOON TOASTED SESAME SEEDS**
1/4 ...... **CUP CORN OIL FOR PANFRYING**

Garnishes

2 ...... **RED AND 2 GREEN SEMI-HOT CHILIES, SEEDED AND CUT INTO THIN, DIAGONAL SLICES**
5 ...... **SCALLIONS, GREEN PART ONLY, CUT INTO 1-INCH PIECES**
2 ...... **TABLESPOONS CHOPPED GARLIC (6 CLOVES)**
2 ...... **TABLESPOONS CHOPPED SCALLIONS, GREEN PART ONLY**

1 Soak the mung beans in water to cover for 4 hours. Drain. Grind the beans in a processor, leaving a little texture. Blanch the bean sprouts in hot water for 3 minutes, drain, and press out the liquid firmly. Set aside. Rinse the cabbage in cold water, drain, and cut into 1/4-inch dice. Press out the liquid.

(Continued next page)

2 Mix the eggs and flour together rather well. Add the processed beans, the bean sprouts, cabbage, beef, garlic, chopped scallion, salt, pepper, sesame oil and sesame seeds and mix.

3 Heat 1 tablespoon oil in a skillet over low heat. Pour out about ½ cup batter, which is rather thick, into a pancake 4 inches in diameter and ¼ inch thick. In a separate bowl, mix together the 2 tablespoons scallions and garlic for seasoning.

4 Place on top of the pancake 4 slices of the semi-hot red and green chilies, 4 slices of scallion and 1 teaspoon of the seasoning mixture. Then dribble 1 teaspoon of the batter over the garnishes to hold them in place as the pancake fries. Fry for 2 or 3 minutes until lightly brown on one side, then turn and cook the other side. Low heat prevents the surface from becoming too dark and yet is enough to cook the pancake and its ingredients through.

Serve warm with a dip made of 3 tablespoons soy sauce, 1 teaspoon chopped garlic, 1 teaspoon chopped scallion, ¼ teaspoon black pepper, 1 teaspoon sesame oil and 1 teaspoon toasted sesame seeds.

Makes 12 pancakes.

NOTE: *If the yellow skinless mung beans are not available, use green mung beans and remove the skins before preparing the pancakes. Soak the beans in water for 4 hours to loosen the green skins and remove them by briskly rubbing the beans together in the water. In this case there is no need to soak again before grinding.*

Pyogo Jon

MUSHROOM AND SHRIMP PANCAKE

Unlimited variations of the *jon*, Korean-style pancakes, are found all over
the country. Frequently, the *jon* are served with mukhuli, the peasant
rice wine that is so good it could lead to addiction. In one traditional eating house on the island of Cheju, I was served a pitcher full of
the mukhuli, cold and refreshing on a scorching day.

> 8 ...... **MEDIUM-SIZE DRIED MUSHROOMS**
> 15 ..... **MEDIUM SHRIMPS, ABOUT ½ POUND,
> PEELED AND DEVEINED**
> 1 ...... **EGG, BEATEN**
> 1 ...... **TEASPOON SALT, OR TO TASTE**
> ½ ..... **CUP WATER**
> ¾ ..... **CUP FLOUR**
> ¼ ..... **CUP CORN OIL**

1 Soak the mushrooms in cold water to cover for 1 hour, or until soft.
Pull out and discard the stems. Press out the liquid quite firmly and
cut the mushrooms into julienne strips.
2 Process the shrimps until smooth, using 1 tablespoon water to
moisten the mixture. Then mix the shrimps, mushrooms, egg, salt,
water and flour together for the batter.
3 Heat the oil in a skillet, scoop out 1 heaping tablespoon of the batter,
and fry a 3-inch pancake over moderate heat until golden on both
sides. Continue with remaining batter.

Serve warm with the Jon Dip.

Makes about 10 pancakes.

Jon Dip II

> 1 ...... **GARLIC CLOVE, CHOPPED FINE**
> 1 ...... **TEASPOON FINE-CHOPPED OR
> CRUSHED FRESH GINGER**
> 2 ...... **SCALLIONS, SLICED ¼ INCH THICK**
> 1 ...... **TABLESPOON KOREAN SESAME OIL**
> 1 ...... **TABLESPOON SESAME SEED SALT**
> ¼ ..... **TEASPOON BLACK PEPPER**

Mix everything together and serve with the pancakes.

Gogi Chun

Meat is expensive and Koreans in general are not big meat-eaters. This side dish of Bean-Curd and Pork Patties takes the best from both worlds, the meat and vegetarian.

- ¼ ..... **POUND GROUND PORK**
- 1 ...... **SQUARE OF SOFT BEAN CURD (TUBU), MASHED, THEN DRIED ON A TOWEL TO REMOVE EXCESS WATER**
- ¼ ..... **TEASPOON SALT**
- 1 ...... **GARLIC CLOVE, CRUSHED**
- 1 ...... **EGG, BEATEN**
- 2 ...... **TABLESPOONS CORN OIL FOR PANFRYING**

1 Mix everything together except the oil. This can be done in a few moments in a processor. Prepare the patties about 2 inches across and ¼ inch thick.

2 Heat the oil in a skillet and lightly brown the patties on both sides over moderate heat for about 3 minutes or until golden. Drain briefly on paper towels.

Serve warm as an appetizer or side dish with other foods. Serve with a soy sauce dip.

Makes 6 patties.

Twigim

Buckwheat flour is especially popular on Cheju Island, but also in some of the other cities, for preparing pancakes and fritters. The ladies cooking fritters in their outdoor stalls at the central market were using buckwheat flour and an egg (for color, they said) and doing a thriving take-out business. They set up a trestle table or two for the public and that was where I sampled various combinations, always searching for new ones. A Korean friend and I had an assortment of these Twigim one day, with a sesame soy dip, radish kimchi and Coca Cola for a total of $2.00.

The Koreans use the real sweet potatoes, not yams.

Batter

1	CUP BUCKWHEAT FLOUR
1/2	TEASPOON SALT
1/8	TEASPOON BAKING POWDER
1	EGG, BEATEN
1/2	CUP WATER OR MORE

Fritters

8 TO 12	MEDIUM SHRIMPS, PEELED AND DEVEINED BUT LEAVING THE TAIL FINS
1/2	CUP CORN OIL FOR PANFRYING
6	WILD SESAME LEAVES (PERILLA) WHERE AVAILABLE, OTHERWISE USE SPINACH LEAVES WITHOUT THE STEMS
6	SWEET POTATO SLICES, ABOUT 1/8 INCH THICK
9	VERY THIN STEAK SLICES, CUT INTO 3-INCH LENGTHS, 1 INCH WIDE
ABOUT 10 ..	THIN SLICES OF FRESH HOT RED CHILI, SEEDED
2	SCALLIONS, GREEN PART ONLY, CUT INTO JULIENNE STRIPS 2 INCHES LONG
1	SMALL CARROT, CUT INTO JULIENNE STRIPS 2 INCHES LONG

1 Prepare the batter. Mix the flour, salt, baking powder, egg, and enough water to prepare a medium-thick batter.

2 Take 2 shrimps at a time and press them together at the heads with the tails sticking outward. Dip these into the batter and put them

(Continued next page)

carefully into 2 tablespoons oil in a skillet over low heat. Care should be taken so that the shrimps do not come apart. To ensure this, dribble an additional teaspoon of batter around the spot where the shrimps are joined together. Fry each pair of shrimps for 3 minutes, turning over once. Drain briefly on paper towels.

3 Dip leaves, one by one, into the batter and fry on both sides for 3 minutes. Add oil when necessary.

4 Dip and fry the sweet potato slices for 3 minutes or a bit longer since they have a firmer texture.

5 Put another tablespoon of oil in the skillet. Dip 3 slices of steak into the batter and place them quickly in the oil, one alongside the other so that you have a pancake about 3 inches square. Push in 2 slices of chili on top of the steak and dribble 1 teaspoon of batter over the top. Fry on both sides for 2 or 3 minutes, just enough to brown lightly.

6 For the scallion and carrot pancake, pour $\frac{1}{4}$ cup of the batter into the oiled skillet. Quickly cover it with about 4 scallion slices and several strips of carrot. (These are imperfect measurements but the idea is to cover the batter completely.) Dribble 1 teaspoon of batter over all and brown on both sides over low heat for 3 minutes.

Serve the twigim warm with a soy sauce dip of your choice. Side dishes of kimchi and pickled radish may be served with these.

Serves 4 to 6.

Cheju-do Haemul Jon

SEAFOOD PANCAKE FROM CHEJU ISLAND

The waters around Cheju Island supply vast amounts of fresh fish and seafood daily, so that these are the principal foods in the Korean diet. This pancake, which I mixed, cooked and tasted on Cheju Island, made use of the local ingredients wisely and well. Buckwheat flour, used more on this island than on the mainland, is the flour of choice in preparing the batter.

2 ...... CUPS BUCKWHEAT FLOUR
1 ...... CUP WATER
½ ..... TEASPOON SALT
¼ ..... CUP THIN-SLICED FRESH SQUID
¼ ..... CUP THIN-SLICED CLAM OR MUSSEL MEAT
2 ...... SCALLIONS, CUT INTO JULIENNE STRIPS 2 INCHES LONG
1 ...... TEASPOON CHOPPED FRESH HOT GREEN CHILI
2 ...... TABLESPOONS JULIENNE-SLICED CARROT
          CORN OIL FOR SKILLET OR GRILL FRYING
4 ...... EGGS, BEATEN

1 Mix the flour, water and salt together into a batter, which should be thin.
2 Mix the squid, clam meat, scallions, chili and carrot together and divide into 4 equal parts.
3 Heat 2 teaspoons oil in a skillet or grill and pour out ¾ cup of the batter into an 8-inch-round pancake. Scatter quickly 1 portion of the seafood mixture over the surface and over this 1 beaten egg.
4 Brown the pancake over low heat for about 3 minutes on each side. Make pancakes with remaining batter and seafood mixture. Cut each pancake into 3 equal slices and serve warm with a dip of choice.

Makes 4 pancakes and could serve 6 persons with other dishes.

Jon

ASSORTED STUFFED FRITTERS

All Koreans love *jon*, those eclectic fritters that can serve as appetizers with drinks or as side dishes with a complete dinner menu. These *jon* include vegetables and seafood, stuffed or not, but panfried in a small amount of oil over low heat for a few minutes so that the color is not the dark brown of deep-frying but the pale golden of the egg. The fritters should not be overcooked since color is an important characteristic of the style of preparation.

There are a great many varieties of *jon*—many in a batter—but those in the following collection are simply enrobed in flour, dipped into beaten egg, and panfried.

Ground Beef Stuffing

1/4	POUND GROUND BEEF
2	TABLESPOONS GRATED CARROT
2	TABLESPOONS CHOPPED ONION
1	SCALLION, CHOPPED FINE
1/2	TEASPOON SALT, OR TO TASTE
1/8	TEASPOON BLACK PEPPER

Ground Beef and Bean-Curd Stuffing

1/4	POUND GROUND BEEF
1	SQUARE OF SOFT BEAN CURD, SLICED, DRIED ON PAPER TOWELS AND MASHED SMOOTHLY
1/2	TEASPOON SALT, OR TO TASTE
1/4	TEASPOON BLACK PEPPER

Fritters

1	MEDIUM-SIZE ONION, ABOUT 2 1/2 INCHES IN DIAMETER, PEELED
1	MEDIUM-SIZE SWEET GREEN (BELL) PEPPER
1	SEMI-HOT GREEN CHILI
4	DRIED MUSHROOMS, ABOUT 2 INCHES IN DIAMETER, SOAKED IN WATER TO COVER FOR 1 HOUR
4	FRESH MUSHROOMS, ABOUT 2 INCHES IN DIAMETER
1/2	POUND FLOUNDER FILLET, OR SIMILAR FISH
	FLOUR FOR DREDGING (ABOUT 1 CUP)

3 . . . . . . EGGS, BEATEN WITH ½ TEASPOON SALT, FOR DIPPING
CORN OIL FOR PANFRYING

1 Make the two stuffings by mixing the proper ingredients together. Keep at hand for stuffing the vegetables.

2 Cut the onion into ¼-inch-thick slices. Remove the 2 inner rings and leave the rest intact. Dust the slice with flour, stuff the center with about 1 heaping teaspoon of either of the beef stuffings, dust again with flour and set aside. There should be 4 or 5 complete stuffed slices.

3 Cut the pepper lengthwise into 6 equal parts. Remove the seeds, ribs and stem. Dust the inside of each slice with flour and stuff with 2 heaping teaspoons of either stuffing. Dust again and set aside.

4 Cut the chili lengthwise into halves; remove the seeds and stem. Dust the inside with flour and stuff each half with 2 teaspoons of either beef stuffing. Set aside.

5 Remove the dried mushrooms from the water and cut off and discard the stems. Dry the caps well, then dust the inside with flour. Stuff each with 2 or 3 heaping teaspoons of either beef mixture. Set aside.

6 Cut the stems off the fresh mushrooms. Rinse the caps well, dry and dust with flour. Stuff with 2 or 3 heaping teaspoons of either beef mixture. Set aside.

7 Cut the fillet into 2½-inch-square pieces. Sprinkle with a few grains of salt on both sides of each piece. Let stand for 20 minutes. Dust each slice with flour and set aside.

8 Heat about 2 tablespoons corn oil in a skillet over low heat. Dredge whatever fritter you wish to prepare with flour and shake off the excess. Then dip into the beaten eggs and add to skillet, frying slowly for about 3 minutes, turning over once. The color should be pale yellow for the fish to a darker cast for the mushrooms and vegetables. Remove the fritters and drain briefly on paper towels.

Serve them arranged in an aesthetic manner with dark and light fritters alternating on the serving platter. Serve warm with a dip made by mixing 2 tablespoons soy sauce, ½ teaspoon cider vinegar, 1 teaspoon sesame oil and ¼ teaspoon toasted sesame seeds.

Serves 4.

Saewoo Twigim

DEEP-FRIED SHRIMPS AND ASSORTED VEGETABLES

A *twigim* is an enormously pleasing Korean mixed fry, using seafood, vegetables and sometimes meat. Usually, there is a wide assortment of all categories with emphasis on colors, which are important in the presentation–the orange of the carrot, the white of the onion, green of zucchini and green pepper, and the purple skin of the eggplant, to name a few. The best way to serve this medley is to serve them at once and eat them while still hot—only possible in a household where there are servants.

When refrigeration was not available, seafood, especially that brought from the coast to interior towns, was vulnerable to spoilage in the hot summers. Because frying food was reputed to kill bacteria, *twigim* became a popular summertime dish.

Shrimps are not the most popular seafood, primarily because of the cost. The families who do serve them to impress their guests make them look as important as possible by the method of preparation. They cut open the thick ends of the peeled shrimps from the back, devein, then with a knife gently tap them along the cut to spread farther open. When battered and fried, this method gives the shrimps the appearance of being larger than they really are. A Korean conceit to entertain guests. Otherwise they fry them in their natural shape.

Batter

- 1 ...... CUP FLOUR
- ¼ ..... CUP GLUTINOUS RICE FLOUR
- ⅛ ..... TEASPOON SALT
- 1 ...... CUP WATER
- 1 ...... EGG, BEATEN

Fritters

- ½ ..... POUND MEDIUM SHRIMPS (ABOUT 15)
- ½ ..... TEASPOON SALT
- 1 ...... SMALL POTATO, PEELED, CUT INTO ROUND SLICES ¼ INCH THICK OR 3-INCH-LONG STICKS
- 1 ...... SMALL ZUCCHINI, CUT INTO 3-INCH-LONG STICKS
- 1 ...... SMALL EGGPLANT, ¼ POUND OR LESS, CUT INTO 3-INCH-LONG STICKS
- 1 ...... MEDIUM-SIZE CARROT, CUT INTO 3-INCH-LONG THIN STICKS
- 1 ...... MEDIUM-SIZE ONION, PEELED, CUT INTO ¼-INCH-WIDE SLICES, WITH 2 CENTER RINGS PUSHED OUT

THE KOREAN KITCHEN

102

1 ...... **SMALL GREEN PEPPER, CUT INTO ¼-INCH-WIDE RINGS**
1 ...... **CUP OR MORE CORN OIL**
2 ...... **SCALLIONS, CUT INTO 3-INCH PIECES**
½ ..... **TEASPOON SALT**
½ ..... **CUP BREAD CRUMBS**

Dip

2 ...... **TABLESPOONS SOY SAUCE**
1 ...... **TEASPOON WHITE OR CIDER VINEGAR**
¼ ..... **TEASPOON KOREAN SESAME OIL**

1 To prepare the batter, mix the flours, salt, water and egg together into a smooth batter. Set aside.
2 Shell all the shrimps to the last segment of the tail which is left intact. For all the shrimps that you have decided are to be fried in their rounded shape, take a needle and plunge it into the back of the shrimp, catch the black vein and pull it out.

Rinse all the shrimps in cold water, drain well, and sprinkle a few grains of salt on each one. Set aside for frying.
3 Sprinkle a few grains of salt over the potato, zucchini and eggplant. The carrots, onion and green pepper are not salted. Set aside.
4 Heat the 1 cup corn oil in a wok or skillet over medium/high heat. Drop a few drops of batter into the hot oil; if they rise and sizzle, the oil is hot enough. All of the *twigim* are quick fried over high heat.

Fry each vegetable separately; dip into the batter, then put into the hot oil and fry for about 2 minutes. Turn them over once. Remove them with a slotted spoon and drain on paper towels. For the scallions, however, hold 3 green stems together, dip them into the batter, then put the bundle into the oil.

The shrimps are treated somewhat differently. The rounded, uncut shrimps are merely dipped into the batter and lightly browned in the hot oil. The shrimps that have been cut are dipped into the batter, then into the bread crumbs and quick fried in the oil. Their size has been further enlarged by the addition of the crumbs.
5 Mix the Dip ingredients together and serve with the hot *twigim*, arranged on a platter in alternating colors and shapes.

Serves 4 to 6.

(Continued next page)

VARIATIONS: Sookgat *(chrysanthemum leaves)*, sesame leaves, *3-inch-long thin slices of steak or breast of chicken, fresh squid sliced in the round, dried mushrooms that have been soaked and drained, fresh halved mushrooms, and sweet potato slices are some of the other items which can be batter-fried in the* twigim *style.*

The batter is also subject to change. The simple batter included in this recipe is the old grandmotherly style. Modern additions to the batter are baking powder and cornstarch, which are thought to create a crisp exterior to the twigim *during frying. Bread crumbs are also an innovation since Koreans in the past were exclusively rice eaters.*

Ehoba Pak Jon

The young tender zucchini are ready in the spring so this dish is also considered a spring preparation. These tender fried slices are often found as one of the side dishes in a Korean meal but they could be served as an appetizer with drinks.

2	**SMALL ZUCCHINI, ½ POUND, CUT INTO ¼-INCH SLICES**
½	**TEASPOON SALT**
2	**TABLESPOONS FLOUR**
	CORN OIL FOR PANFRYING
2	**EGGS, BEATEN WITH ½ TEASPOON SALT**

1 Sprinkle the squash slices with salt and let stand for 10 minutes. Toss them with flour.
2 Heat the oil in a wok or skillet. Dip the slices into the beaten eggs and fry over moderate heat for 1 minute so that they retain their crunch. Turn the slices over just once. Drain briefly on paper towels.

Serve warm with a dip made of 2 tablespoons soy sauce, 1 teaspoon white vinegar, 1 teaspoon toasted sesame seeds. Mix well.

Serves 4.

VARIATION: *Eggplant, cucumber, thin-sliced sweet potato may also be prepared in the same manner as the squash. The sweet potato needs a little longer than the others to cook through.*

Soe Gan Jon

BEEF OR VEAL LIVER FRITTER

Liver is an expensive meat in Korea—a fact my Korean friend explained by calling to my attention that in the big body of a cow there is only a small liver. Also liver is a highly desirable meat from the health point of view since it is loaded with vitamin A and is considered as good as a medicine. These fritters are as tasty as they are unusual and can be enjoyed for several reasons.

1 ...... POUND BEEF OR VEAL LIVER, IN ONE PIECE
3 ...... CUPS WATER
2 ...... TEASPOONS SALT
½ ..... INCH OF FRESH GINGER, SLICED
2 ...... FRESH BURDOCK ROOTS, SCRAPED, WELL RINSED, CHOPPED (OPTIONAL, SEE NOTE)
4 .... SEMI-HOT GREEN CHILIES, SEEDED, CHOPPED
1 ...... CARROT, CHOPPED (½ CUP)
½ ..... TEASPOON PEPPER
¼ ..... CUP CHOPPED SCALLION
1 ...... TABLESPOON CHOPPED GARLIC
1½ ..... TABLESPOONS SOY SAUCE
½ ..... CUP FLOUR
1 ...... EGG, BEATEN
      CORN OR SOYBEAN OIL FOR PANFRYING

1 Rinse the liver well in cold water. Drain. Bring to a boil 3 cups water, 1 teaspoon of the salt, the ginger and the liver. Simmer over moderate heat for 15 minutes. Drain, cool, and chop the liver.

2 Mix the liver, burdock if used, chilies, carrot, pepper, scallion, garlic, soy sauce and 1 tablespoon of the flour into a fritter mixture.

3 Shape fritters 2 inches across and ½ inch thick. Coat them with flour, then with egg. Heat the oil in a skillet and fry the fritter over moderate heat for 1 minute on each side, or until golden brown. Drain on paper towels.

Serve warm with rice, kimchi and a dip of your choice.

Makes 12 fritters.

NOTE: *Burdock* (Arctium lappa) *is also known as* gobo *or Japanese burdock. The roots are scraped and well rinsed in cold water to eliminate bitterness. Although they do not have much flavor, the roots are used in the fritter because they remove the strong liver aroma.*

Goon Mandu

Many cultures take ground meat and vegetables, enrobe them in a dumpling or pancake and then fry, steam or bake them. The Koreans have their own special seasoning and technique of assembly and their dumplings take second place to none. The egg whites, white flour and starch keep the wrapper white as they like it, and the golden yolks enrich the filling. Regardless of the cooking method, whether steam-frying as in this case, or steaming in a Chinese-style steamer, a garlic-laden soy sauce dip provides the fire.

Filling

- 1 ...... POUND GROUND LEAN BEEF
- 1/4 ..... POUND CHINESE CHIVES
- 1 ...... SMALL ONION, CHOPPED FINE (1/2 CUP)
- 1/4 ..... POUND BEAN SPROUTS, BLANCHED IN BOILING WATER FOR 10 SECONDS, DRAINED THOROUGHLY, CHOPPED FINE AND ALL LIQUID PRESSED OUT
- 2 ...... UNBEATEN EGG YOLKS (KEEP WHITES FOR DOUGH)
- 1/4 ..... INCH OF FRESH GINGER, CHOPPED FINE
- 2 ...... TABLESPOONS CORNSTARCH
- 1 ...... TEASPOON SALT, OR TO TASTE
- 1/4 ..... TEASPOON PEPPER
- 2 ...... TEASPOONS KOREAN SESAME OIL
- 1 ...... TEASPOON TOASTED SESAME SEEDS

Dough

- 3 1/2 .... CUPS FLOUR
- 1/4 ..... CUP CORNSTARCH
- 3/4 ..... CUP BOILING WATER
- 2 ...... EGG WHITES
- 2/3 ..... CUP COLD WATER (ABOUT), IN WHICH 1/2 TEASPOON SALT IS DISSOLVED
- 1 ...... BEATEN EGG FOR SEALING
- CORN OIL AND 1 TEASPOON KOREAN SESAME OIL FOR PANFRYING
- 2 ...... TABLESPOONS COLD WATER

(Continued next page)

1 To make the filling, put the beef in a large mixing bowl. Cut off the white part of the chives and discard. Cut the green stems into thin slices. Add to the mixing bowl with the onion, bean sprouts, egg yolks, ginger, cornstarch, salt, pepper, sesame oil and seeds. Mix well.

2 Roll 1 tablespoon of the filling into a ball about 1 inch in diameter. Prepare all the filling this way and refrigerate. There should be about 25 meatballs.

3 Mix 3 cups of the flour, the cornstarch and boiling water together as well as possible. Add the egg whites and enough cold water to make a soft, perhaps even slightly sticky, but manageable dough. Put the dough in a plastic bag and refrigerate for 1/2 to 1 hour.

4 Remove the dough from the refrigerator. Flour a kitchen board generously with the reserved 1/2 cup, since the soft dough may be somewhat sticky. Roll out the dough into 1 or 2 long sausages about 1 1/2 inches in diameter. Cut it into 1-inch slices to prepare individual dumplings.

5 Roll out each slice of dough into an oval, about 3 by 4 inches. Prepare all the skins this way. Moisten one edge of the skin with the beaten egg and place 1 slightly flattened filling ball in the center. Fold over the skin into a half-moon to meet the egg-dabbed end. Pinch the ends together to seal. Prepare all the dumplings this way and dust them with flour.

6 Heat the corn and sesame oil over low heat in a covered skillet that will contain about 10 dumplings. Add the dumplings to the oil with the flat side down. Cover the pan and fry for 1 minute. Turn them over; they should be light brown. Add the water and quickly cover the pan. Fry/steam for 2 or 3 minutes until all the water has evaporated as the sizzling stops (see Note). Remove the dumplings to a serving platter and continue with the remainder of skins and fillings in the same way. (This recipe may be halved if desired.)

Serve warm with the dip.

Makes 25 dumplings.

Dip

3 ...... **TABLESPOONS SOY SAUCE**
5 ...... **PINE NUTS, CRUSHED**
1 ...... **TEASPOON FINE-CHOPPED GARLIC**
1/4 ..... **TEASPOON SESAME OIL**

Mix everything together and serve at room temperature.

(Continued next page)

VARIATION: Pheasant Stuffing: *For a very special dumpling filling, the Koreans turn to the wild pheasant. Nowadays, pheasants are not so wild since they are raised in Korea in pens on the island of Cheju. The farm-raised pheasant is also available in special meat markets in New York and other cities.*

For this filling, omit the ground beef and substitute 1 soft soybean cake (tubu) and ½ pound ground pheasant meat, both light and dark. Mash the soybean cake and wring it out firmly in a cloth kitchen towel to remove excess liquid. Mix with the pheasant and proceed with ingredients and instructions for beef stuffing. The slightly gamey flavor is enjoyed by Koreans for birthdays and other special occasions.

NOTE: *If you prefer to steam the dumplings without frying, use a Chinese-style steamer with a double thickness of cheesecloth on each shelf. Place the dumplings on the cloth over boiling water and steam over moderate heat for 20 minutes.*

Yang Yeum Kanjang

SEASONED DIPPING SAUCE

½ ..... CUP SOY SAUCE

½ ..... TEASPOON KOREAN SESAME OIL

½ ..... TEASPOON TOASTED SESAME SEEDS, CRUSHED IN A MORTAR

1 ...... TEASPOON THIN-SLICED SCALLION

¼ ..... TEASPOON HOT RED CHILI POWDER (*GOCHU GARU,* OPTIONAL)

¼ ...... TEASPOON SUGAR

⅛ ..... TEASPOON WHITE PEPPER

Mix everything together thoroughly and serve when wanted. The sauce may be stored in the refrigerator for 1 week.

Makes about ½ cup sauce.

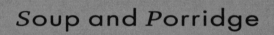

Soup and Porridge

Soup is a frequent if not daily item on the Korean table. It might be a cold broth served as a side dish or a more complex soup of beef, fish or seafood, noodles and vegetables. The frigid winters in the northern part of Korea encourage dining on hot soups, spiced with traditional seasonings. "Soups Unlimited" might be the way to describe the variety and popularity of soup.

This is not to imply that soup is served only during the cold weather. There are cold soups with noodles and beef that are considered an excellent lunch. There are exceptional soups for uncommon occasions such as the one in which ginseng is cooked with baby chicken, or the soup for a hangover. The more substantial soups are packed with seafood and noodles or include the familiar stuffed dumpling (won ton) in a heady beef broth. Another type is a clear broth with an almost neutral taste which is used as a side dish.

All of the soups have one thing in common in that they are based on water—not milk—and are almost fat free. A soup should exalt health, strength, thrift and good taste.

Korean porridges are like thick soups, rely on good taste, of course, but often also rely on a purpose. The ones included in this collection will, we believe, renew lost energy and promote good health. We in the West can enjoy them for their good taste and ease of preparation.

Mandu Kook

The beef-stuffed dumplings (similar to won ton) are traditionally served in a hot and potent beef broth with several garnishes. The commercial dumplings (Chinese won ton or Korean *mandu*) are available in Asian groceries.

> 15 ..... CUPS BOILING WATER
> 2 ...... POUNDS BEEF BONES SUCH AS SHIN BONES AND RIBS
> 1 ...... TEASPOON SALT
> ½ ...... INCH OF FRESH GINGER, SLICED THIN
> 1 ...... EGG, SEPARATED
> 4 TO 6 ... DUMPLINGS (MANDU) PER PERSON
> 2 ...... SCALLIONS, SLICED THIN DIAGONALLY
> ½ ...... CUP TOASTED LAVER, SHREDDED TO THIN 2-INCH LENGTHS

1 Put the water, bones, salt and ginger into a large pan, bring to a boil and skim off and discard the foam that accumulates. Cook over moderate heat for 2 to 3 hours. About half of the liquid will evaporate during this time, leaving a strong broth. Remove and discard the bones and ginger. Taste and adjust the amount of salt.

2 Prepare 2 small omelets, one with the white and one with the yolk. Cool and slice into thin 2-inch lengths. Set aside.

3 Simmer the dumplings in the beef broth for about 10 minutes. Serve hot in individual bowls, 4 to 6 dumplings per person or more if wanted, garnished with the omelet pieces, scallions and laver shreds. Or serve in one large family-style tureen.

Serves 6 to 8.

Kom Tang

BEEF BONE SOUP

Knuckle bones are not the most desirable part of the animal but they produce a broth extremely rich in flavor. The bones, which should have some meat attached, and the translucent cartilage have a character all their own. I have been served the tender bones as a separate dish as well as the broth and the meat parts as a complete soup. Some restaurants do serve Bone Soup (Kom Tang) but it is essentially home cooking and is served all over Korea.

8 ...... CUPS WATER
3 TO 5 ... BEEF KNUCKLES WITH MEAT AND CARTILAGE ATTACHED, WELL RINSED
1 ...... CARROT, HALVED LENGTHWISE
1 ...... MEDIUM-SIZE ONION, HALVED
1 ...... KOREAN RADISH, PEELED AND CUT INTO A 4-INCH PIECE
1 ...... TEASPOON SALT, OR TO TASTE
5 ...... SCALLIONS, SLICED THIN
1 ...... TEASPOON TOASTED SESAME SEEDS
1 ...... TEASPOON HOT CHILI POWDER
1 ...... TEASPOON CHOPPED FRESH GINGER

1 Bring the water, bones, carrot, onion and radish to a boil over high heat for 20 minutes. Skim off and discard the foam. Reduce the heat to low and simmer, covered, for 2 hours, which should be sufficient to tenderize the ingredients.

2 Remove the bones from the broth; cut off the meat and cartilage and cut into ½-inch cubes. Discard the carrot and onion.

3 Slice the radish into thin 1-inch squares. Add to the hot broth with the meat pieces, salt, scallions, sesame seeds, hot chili powder and ginger. Mix briskly and serve immediately.

Serves 8 to 10.

Marun Saeoo

Small, bright pink or orange, plump dried shrimps may be found in Asian
and Latin American food shops. They provide a seafood essence quite
different from fresh shrimps. This consommé at serving time is garnished with several leaves of crisp, green watercress.

6 ...... CUPS WATER

**2 ...... GENEROUS TABLESPOONS
DRIED SHRIMPS**

1 ...... SMALL CARROT, HALVED LENGTHWISE

1 ...... SMALL ONION, HALVED

**1 ...... KOREAN RADISH, PEELED AND CUT
INTO A 2-INCH PIECE**

1 ...... TABLESPOON TOASTED SESAME SEEDS

1 ...... TEASPOON HOT CHILI POWDER

1 ...... TEASPOON CHOPPED FRESH GINGER

1 ...... TEASPOON SALT, OR TO TASTE

**WATERCRESS (YOUNG STEMS AND
LEAVES) FOR GARNISH**

1 Bring the water to a boil in a large pan, add the shrimps, carrot,
onion, radish, sesame seeds, chili powder, ginger and salt. Cook
rapidly for 5 minutes, then reduce the heat to low and simmer for
20 minutes.
2 Strain the broth and discard all the vegetables and seasonings.
Serve hot in bowls garnished with several watercress sprigs.

Serves 6 to 8.

Miyuk Kook

Although this soup is tasty and healthful for anyone at any time, Korean women have, for generations, sipped Miyuk Kook to revive their flagging energy after the birth of a child. The traditional mother will drink the soup 3 times daily for 7 weeks as assistance to her recovery. It is eaten by all classes of society from royalty to peasant and is served to the woman on her birthdays in later years. A failure to dine on this birthday soup would indicate a lack of discipline. Does the modern young Korean woman partake of this ancient health restorer? Some do and some don't but probably not to the extent of their grandmothers.

Miyuk is a special brown seaweed (*Undaria pinnatifida*) that possesses the restorative properties found in the soup.

6...... **OUNCES DRIED MIYUK SEAWEED**
1...... **TABLESPOON KOREAN SESAME OIL**
½..... **POUND FRESH OYSTERS, DRAINED**
1...... **TEASPOON SALT**
7...... **CUPS BOILING WATER**

1 Soak the seaweed in cold water for about 20 minutes or until flexible. Drain and tear it into 3- or 4-inch-long strips.
2 Heat the sesame oil in a large pan; add the seaweed, oysters and salt. Stir-fry over moderate heat for 1 minute to firm the oysters. The seaweed will turn dark green, which was its original fresh color.
3 Add the boiling water to the pan and simmer over moderate heat, covered, for 7 to 8 minutes. Adjust the salt if necessary.

Serve hot with rice.

Serves 6.

Tubu Kook

SIMPLE BEAN-CURD SOUP

A number of the Korean soups used to accompany the meal are prepared with simple ingredients and without spices or heavy seasonings. The aim is a "clean," natural flavor.

- **3½..... CUPS WATER**
- **1 ...... MEDIUM-SIZE ONION, SLICED (½CUP)**
- **1 ...... SOFT BEAN CURD, CUT INTO 1-INCH CUBES**
- **½ ..... CUP JULIENNE SLICED BAMBOO SHOOTS (CANNED)**
- **1 ...... SCALLION, CUT INTO 1-INCH PIECES**
- **4 ...... TABLESPOONS GROUND DRIED ANCHOVY**

Bring the water to a boil in a pan, add all the other ingredients, and simmer over moderate heat, covered, for 15 minutes.

Serve hot during the Korean meal.

Serves 4.

NOTE: *Bamboo shoots are infrequently encountered fresh in Asian markets in the United States. The canned are always available and perfectly acceptable.*

The dried, ground anchovy powder can be purchased in small packages in Korean groceries; it adds a seafood flavor to the soup.

Wanja Tang

MEATBALL SOUP

The broth in this soup is mild, clean-tasting and flavored by the meatball seasonings. An optional choice is to use home-cooked beef broth in place of water, which will strengthen the soup and give it more intensity of flavor.

½ ..... **POUND GROUND LEAN BEEF**
½ ..... **SQUARE SOFT SOYBEAN CURD, SQUEEZED DRY IN A TOWEL, THEN MASHED**
1 ...... **SCALLION, CHOPPED**
½ ..... **TEASPOON SALT**
⅛ ..... **TEASPOON PEPPER**
2 ...... **CUPS WATER OR BEEF BROTH**
1 ...... **EGG, BEATEN**
¼ ..... **TEASPOON ASIAN SESAME OIL**

1 Mix together the ground beef, bean curd, scallion, salt and pepper and prepare meatballs ¾ inch in diameter.

2 Bring the water to a boil in a pan over moderate heat. When the water boils, dip the meatballs, one at a time, into the beaten egg and drop them into the water. When the liquid boils again the meatballs will float, indicating that they are almost cooked. Simmer for 10 minutes more. Now add the sesame oil. Adjust the salt if necessary.

Serve hot, soup and meatballs together.

Serves 2 or 3.

Beuseus Denjang Jeege

SPICED MUSHROOM STEW

This mushroom soup is a great favorite. Flavored with the bean paste and other common and plentiful ingredients, it is delicious yet simple and easy to prepare.

10 ..... **DRIED MUSHROOMS**
3 ...... **CUPS WATER**
2 ...... **TABLESPOONS DENJANG BEAN PASTE**
4 ...... **GARLIC CLOVES, CHOPPED FINE**
6 ...... **SCALLIONS, BOTH GREEN AND WHITE PARTS, CUT INTO 1-INCH PIECES**

1 Rinse the mushrooms, then cover with 3 cups water and let them soak for 1 hour, or until soft. Shred the mushroom caps to thin slices; discard the stems. Reserve the mushroom liquid, adding more water if necessary to make 3 cups.

2 Bring the liquid and bean paste to a boil in a pan and simmer over low heat, covered, for 10 minutes. Add the mushrooms, garlic and scallions. Bring to a boil again and simmer for 5 minutes.

Serve warm with rice.

Serves 4.

On Myon

Korean soups occasionally have small amounts of beef to give the broth more strength. But the meat is subordinate to the soup itself, which ultimately focuses on the vegetables and noodles for its interest. We use here the very thin, white, round Japanese wheat noodles that are available in any Korean grocery. They literally take only a few seconds in boiling water to cook *al dente*, following the directions on the package.

3	**TEASPOONS CORN OIL**
1	**MEDIUM-SIZE ONION, CUT INTO 2-INCH-LONG SLICES, MORE OR LESS**
10	**CHINESE CHIVES, CUT INTO 2-INCH-LONG PIECES**
2	**SCALLIONS, CUT INTO 2-INCH-LONG PIECES**
1	**SMALL ZUCCHINI (1/4 POUND), CUT INTO JULIENNE STRIPS**
1/2	**TEASPOON SALT**
1/4	**POUND RIB OR SIRLOIN STEAK, CUT INTO 1-INCH JULIENNE STRIPS**
3	**CUPS WATER**
1/4	**TEASPOON PEPPER**
1	**BUNDLE OF JAPANESE THIN WHEAT NOODLES (2 OUNCES)**
1	**EGG, BEATEN**

1 Heat 2 teaspoons of the oil in a skillet and stir-fry the onion, chives, scallions and zucchini for 2 minutes, to partially cook them. During the frying sprinkle with the salt. Set aside.

2 Stir-fry the steak in a soup pan without oil over low heat until the color changes. Add the water and bring to a boil. Remove the dark foam that rises. Now add all the stir-fried vegetables, cover the pan, and simmer over low heat for 5 minutes. Adjust the salt at this time and add the pepper.

3 In another pan, cook the noodles. Cover the pan for a few seconds, bring the water to a boil, then rinse the noodles under cold water. Set aside.

4 Heat the balance of the oil (about 1 teaspoon) in a skillet and pour in the egg to prepare a large pancake. Fry over moderate heat for 1 minute, turn over and fry the other side for a few seconds. Remove and spread the pancake flat to cool. Then fold it in half and cut into thin slices for the garnish.

5 To serve the soup, divide the noodles among 4 soup bowls. Pour in the hot soup with its vegetables and beef, and garnish with the egg slices. Serve hot.

Serves 4.

VARIATION: *The egg garnish may also be prepared by making separate pancakes of egg white and yolk. Koreans like the contrasting colors of white and gold, and egg garnishes are often prepared in this way.*

Miyuk

A country with a coastline as long as the mountainous but seagirt Korean peninsula is a naturally rich source for seaweed. Families living near the shore gather the long strands of seaweed and dry it. A Korean friend living in New York still carries on the tradition by collecting a supply on Long Island during the summer and drying it for yearlong use. However, it can be purchased from Korean groceries, neatly packaged in plastic bags and ready to be used.

2...... **TABLESPOONS DRIED SEAWEED PIECES**
1...... **TEASPOON ASIAN SESAME OIL**
2...... **OUNCES FLANK STEAK, SLICED VERY THIN**
1...... **GARLIC CLOVE, CRUSHED**
2...... **CUPS WATER**
3...... **SCALLIONS, GREEN PART ONLY, CUT INTO 3-INCH PIECES**

1 Cover the seaweed with warm water in a bowl and let the pieces expand for 20 minutes. Rinse and drain.
2 Put the sesame oil in a pan, add the meat and stir-fry over moderate heat for 1 minute. Add the seaweed and garlic and fry for another minute. Add the water, bring to a boil, and add the scallions. Simmer over low heat for 10 minutes.

Serve hot in bowls.

Serves 4.

Yukgeh Jang

BEEF SHREDS AND VEGETABLE SOUP

Koreans dote on fiddlehead fern, especially when it is fresh and the fronds
are emerging from the ground in moist wooded forests. The flavor is
subtle but enhanced considerably with chili and garlic. Cooked without oil or fat, the soup is a fine example of Korean cuisine where the
natural flavors have precedence and are paramount in the character
of the soup.

9 . . . . . . **CUPS WATER**

1/2 . . . . . **POUND FLANK STEAK, IN ONE PIECE**

1/2 . . . . . **TEASPOON SALT**

1/2 . . . . . **POUND BEAN SPROUTS**

10 . . . . . **SCALLIONS, HALVED HORIZONTALLY**

1 . . . . . . **POUND FRESH FERN, HALVED
HORIZONTALLY**

3 . . . . . . **GARLIC CLOVES, CRUSHED**

3 . . . . . . **TEASPOONS HOT RED CHILI POWDER,
OR MORE TO TASTE**

1 . . . . . . **TABLESPOON FLOUR**

1 Bring the water to a boil over moderate heat; add the steak and
salt. Cover the pan and cook for 1/2 hour. Add the bean sprouts and
cook for 10 minutes more. Remove the steak, cool, and pull apart
into shreds about 1/4 inch thick. Set aside.

2 Now add the scallions and fern to the meat broth and cook for 10
minutes. Remove them to a bowl. Add the garlic, chili and flour (for
thickening) to the fern and scallions and mix well. Return this mixture to the broth.

3 Add the steak shreds, bring to a boil, and simmer over low heat
for 1 hour. Adjust the salt. (Some cooks let the soup steep over low
heat for 2 hours.)

Serve hot with white sticky rice. This is a family-style soup served in
the summer. The feeling is that hot soup is "cooling" on hot days.

Serves 8.

Jogae Tang

CLAM AND VEGETABLE SOUP

An assortment of vegetables, including hot chilies, onion and scallions, enriches this soup. The clams are small—about the size of a quarter. It may be easier for us to find the larger local clams that are available most of the year but the smaller, the better.

- **2** ...... **CUPS WATER**
- **1** ...... **SMALL POTATO, PEELED, CUT INTO ¼-INCH-THICK SLICES**
- **1** ...... **MEDIUM-SIZE ONION, SLICED (½ CUP)**
- **2** ...... **GARLIC CLOVES, CRUSHED TO A PASTE**
- **1 OR 2** ... **SEMI-HOT, FRESH GREEN CHILIES, TO TASTE, SEEDED, SLICED THIN**
- **2** ...... **OUNCES BEEFSTEAK, CUT INTO THIN CUBES**
- **6** ...... **SMALL CLAMS (1 TO 2 INCHES), WELL SCRUBBED**
- **1** ...... **SOFT BEAN CURD, CUT INTO 1-INCH CUBES**
- **2** ...... **SCALLIONS, CUT INTO 2-INCH PIECES**
- **1** ...... **TEASPOON SOY SAUCE**
- **½** ...... **TEASPOON SALT**
- **1** ...... **BUNCH (2 OUNCES) FRESH CHRYSANTHEMUM SHOOTS, THICK STEMS TRIMMED (OPTIONAL)**

1 Bring the water to a boil in a pan, add the potato, onion, garlic, chilies and beef and cook over moderate heat for 10 minutes.

2 Add the clams, bean curd, scallions, soy sauce and salt and continue to cook for 5 minutes more. This should be enough to soften the vegetables and integrate the seasonings. Now add the chrysanthemum shoots if used, cover the pan, and remove it from the heat. Let stand for 10 minutes, then serve warm.

Serves 4 with steamed white rice.

Sundubu

Small clams the size of a quarter or smaller are a principal seasoning item for this thick soup. The soup also illustrates the Korean penchant for combining a few ounces of beefsteak with seafood to strengthen the broth and provide another texture. There is no oil or fat here, which has become a relevant criterion for our time. This recipe is from the old city of Kyongju in southeast Korea where I spent several fascinating days researching the cuisine and archeology.

1 ...... SOFT BEAN CURD, COARSELY MASHED OR CHOPPED

¼ ..... CUP SLICED SCALLIONS (2), GREEN PART ONLY

12 ..... SMALL CLAMS IN THE SHELL, OR 6 MEDIUM-SIZE CLAMS

⅔ ..... CUP ANCHOVY WATER

2 ...... OUNCES BEEFSTEAK, CUT INTO JULIENNE STRIPS

½ ..... TEASPOON SALT

1 ...... TEASPOON DRIED HOT RED CHILI FLAKES

Put everything into a pan, bring to a boil, and simmer over low heat for 10 minutes.

Serve hot with rice, side dishes of kimchi and stir-fried vegetable dishes of your choice.

Serves 4.

Denjang Jiege Keh

SPICED CRAB SOUP

The people of Kwangju where this recipe originates like their food salty and chili-hot. The fermented denjang paste provides the basis of the seasonings, aided by the chili and ginger. The fresh crabs absorb the flavors and the entire soup is enormously attractive. I went to my teacher's house one August in the middle of a three day pre-typhoon downpour. Sheets of water poured out of the sky as my taxi wended its way to the edge of town. The rice fields in this rice-growing region shimmered with an intense green as the rain engulfed the paddy. It had a wild, wet beauty but I was glad when I arrived and could concentrate in comfort on the crabs and the soup.

2 ...... CUPS WATER

2 ...... TABLESPOONS DENJANG PASTE

1 ...... SOFT BEAN CURD, CUT INTO
½-INCH CUBES

1 ...... TEASPOON HOT RED CHILI POWDER
WELL MIXED WITH 1 TABLESPOON WATER

1 ...... SLICE OF GINGER, THE SIZE OF
A QUARTER

1 ...... SMALL ONION, SLICED (⅓ CUP)

1 ...... GARLIC CLOVE, CRUSHED

2 ...... CRABS, EACH CUT INTO 4 PIECES

½ ..... CUP SLICED ZUCCHINI

1 Put the water and bean paste (denjang) into a pan and simmer over low heat, covered, for 10 minutes. Add the bean curd and cook for 5 minutes more.

2 Now add all the other ingredients and cook for 15 minutes more. Serve in 4 individual bowls with rice and an assortment of side dishes.

Serves 4.

Saeng Sun Jigae

CHILI-HOT FISH SOUP

In the antique city of Kyongju, the tombs of past emperors rise up on streets all over the city. While there, I walked into a small eating house near my hotel and found myself the only westerner present—as usual. The owner, a young woman, was happy to take me to her kitchen and demonstrate how to make this popular soup. During lunch, I was offered wild sesame leaves to make a table sandwich—with rice, a hot sauce and a mushroom side dish. The leaves have a mild aromatic flavor, perhaps of cinnamon or anise, and are beloved by the Koreans. They are distantly related to the sesame plant that provides the seeds.

½ ..... **POUND WHOLE SEA FISH WITH HEAD (USE RED SNAPPER, PORGY, BUTTERFISH)**

2 ...... **SCALLIONS, SLICED THIN**

1 ...... **MEDIUM-SIZE ONION, SLICED (½ CUP)**

⅓ ..... **CUP HALF-MOON ZUCCHINI SLICES**

1 ...... **TEASPOON HOT RED CHILI FLAKES TO TASTE**

½ ..... **TEASPOON SALT**

1 ...... **CUP ANCHOVY WATER**

1 ...... **GARLIC CLOVE, CRUSHED TO A PASTE**

Put everything into a pan, bring to a boil and cook, covered, over moderate heat for 15 to 20 minutes.

Serve hot with rice, kimchi and salads.

Serves 2 or 3 as a side dish.

Jaechup Kook

CLAM SOUP FOR A HANGOVER

Here is a simple, lightly flavored soup, a soothing broth that is alleged to cure any excessive indulgences of the night before. The baby clams, known as *chechi*, are always available in Korea and are used for flavoring various kinds of soup. The clams are frequently found in New York, and other Asian Shopping Districts, but any small clams may be substituted.

2 ...... CUPS WATER
1 ...... CUP BABY CLAMS, WELL SCRUBBED
¼ ..... CUP SLICED CHINESE CHIVES

Put the water in a pan and bring to a boil. Add the clams and chives and simmer over low heat for 15 minutes.

Serve hot.

Serves 2.

Kalgooksu

Titles of Korean foods often reveal the technique involved, as in this recipe, where the word *kalgooksu* (knife-cut noodles) shows that the noodles were prepared at home, as in the past, and cut into long thin strips, by hand, with a sharp knife.

Kalgooksu is a great favorite in southern Korea because of the anchovy flavor and the overall piquancy of the broth, provided by the beef, chili, clam meat and soy sauce. Purely Korean.

Noodles

- 3 .... CUPS FLOUR
- 1 .... EGG, BEATEN
- 1 .... TEASPOON SALT
  ABOUT ¾ CUP WATER

Soup

- 8 TO 10... CUPS WATER
- 20 ..... DRIED ANCHOVIES, 2½ INCHES LONG, OPENED LENGTHWISE
- 1½..... TABLESPOONS PLUS ¼ CUP SOY SAUCE
- 1 ...... POUND ZUCCHINI, CUT LENGTHWISE INTO HALVES, THEN INTO HALF-MOONS ¼ INCH THICK
- 2 ...... SCALLIONS, WHITE PART ONLY, CUT INTO 3-INCH LENGTHS, HALVED DIAGONALLY
- ½ ..... POUND BEEFSTEAK, CUT INTO 1-INCH STRIPS
- ½ ..... POUND CLAM MEAT, CHOPPED (SEE NOTE)
- 2 ...... SEMI-HOT RED CHILIES, SEEDED, SLICED THIN DIAGONALLY
- 1 ...... TABLESPOON SESAME OIL
- 2 ..... TABLESPOONS TOASTED SESAME SEEDS
- ¼ ..... TEASPOON PEPPER
- 3 ...... GARLIC CLOVES, CHOPPED
- 2 ...... TABLESPOONS CHOPPED SCALLIONS, GREEN PART ONLY
- 1 ...... TEASPOON HOT RED CHILI POWDER

(Continued next page)

1 To prepare the noodles, mix the flour, egg, salt and enough water to form a smooth, malleable dough. Let it rest, covered, for $1/2$ hour. Then roll the dough out into 3 or 4 round pancakes about $1/8$ inch thick. With a sharp knife, slice long, straight strands not more than $1/8$ inch wide. There should be about 2 pounds noodles; store in plastic bags to ensure flexibility. Of course, you may also save time by buying the noodles in an Asian grocery.

2 Bring the water for the soup to a boil in a large pan. Add the anchovies and simmer over low heat for 10 minutes, which will tint the water a pale yellow. This will extract the seafood flavor and provide the base for the soup. Strain the broth and discard the anchovies.

3 Return broth to the pan with $1\frac{1}{2}$ tablespoons soy sauce and the noodles. Bring to a boil and stir over low heat for 10 minutes to separate the noodles and prevent them from sticking to the bottom of the pan. Add the zucchini and the white part of the scallions and simmer for 3 minutes more. The zucchini should have crunch and texture. Set aside.

4 Mix together the steak, clam meat, chili, the $1/4$ cup soy sauce, the sesame oil and seeds, pepper, garlic, chopped scallion greens and red chili powder. Put all this into a skillet and stir-fry over moderate heat for 2 minutes. Set aside.

Serve the soup and the seasoning mélange separately. Each diner will garnish his soup and noodles with the seasoning mix according to his taste.

Serve warm.

Serves 6.

NOTE: *Clam meat is sold frozen in Korean shops; use this for an easy method of obtaining clams to complete the recipe.*

Kimchi Jiege

KIMCHI AND PORK SOUP

Cabbage Pickle may be the most popular side dish in Korean dining but it also serves as a perfect accompaniment to pork. Not only is the fermented cabbage/chili flavor potent, but it gives the bonus of the crisp texture of the cabbage, contrasting nicely with the pork.

2 ...... **CUPS WATER**

½ ..... **POUND HOMEMADE CABBAGE PICKLE, SLICED**

¼ ..... **POUND BONELESS PORK, CUT INTO ¼-INCH DICE**

⅛ ..... **TEASPOON BLACK PEPPER**

1 ...... **SCALLION, SLICED THIN**

1 ...... **SMALL FRESH SEMI-HOT GREEN CHILI, SLICED THIN, RINSED IN COLD WATER TO REMOVE SEEDS**

1 ...... **TEASPOON TOASTED SESAME SEEDS**

10 ..... **DRIED RED CHILI THREADS, AS GARNISH**

1 Put the water and kimchi in a pan, bring to a boil, add the pork and simmer over low heat for 20 minutes. Add water if the liquid evaporates too quickly.

2 Now add the pepper, scallions and fresh chili and cook for another 10 minutes. Remove from the heat and serve in 4 individual bowls. Garnish each bowl with the sesame seeds and chili threads.

Serve warm with rice and favorite side dishes.

Serves 4.

Kimchi Jigae

When the Baechu Kimchi (Cabbage Pickle, see p. 28-29) has matured a little too long in the refrigerator, let us say about two weeks, then it is the ideal time to prepare this soup. Filled with a piquant flavor and enriched with pork, clams and soybean curd, the soup becomes a one-dish meal served with steamed white rice. Pork is the most compatible and traditional meat with the kimchi, although one could use beef. Note that salt, chili or other seasonings are not included since the fermented kimchi supplies all the seasoning it needs.

$1/2$ ...... **TEASPOON KOREAN SESAME OIL**

1 ...... **CUP CABBAGE PICKLE (SEE P. 28-29)**

1 ...... **GARLIC CLOVE, CRUSHED**

$1/4$ ...... **POUND BONELESS PORK, SLICED THIN**

3 ...... **CUPS WATER**

1 ...... **SCALLION, CUT INTO 3-INCH PIECES**

1 ...... **FIRM CHINESE SOYBEAN CURD, CUT INTO 9 CUBES**

6 TO 8 ... **SMALL CLAMS, OPTIONAL BUT RECOMMENDED**

1 Put the sesame oil in a saucepan and stir-fry the kimchi over moderate heat for $1/2$ minute. Add the garlic and pork and continue to fry as the meat changes color.

2 Now add the water, bring to a boil, and cook for 10 minutes. Add the scallion, bean curd, and clams if used, and simmer over low heat for 10 minutes more.

Serve warm with rice.

Serves 4.

Dak Kalgusku

CHICKEN SHREDS IN NOODLE SOUP

Preparing noodles used to be a standard kitchen activity in rural Korean homes. Today one usually buys them in small shops and supermarkets, neatly packaged in round bundles. But I did see a cook in a small Korean eating house in a provincial town running the dough through an electric pasta machine that could turn out quantities at any time.

1 ½	**POUNDS CHICKEN PARTS**
8	**CUPS WATER OR CHICKEN BROTH**
2	**TEASPOONS SALT, OR TO TASTE**
2 TO 3	**TABLESPOONS CHILI POWDER, TO TASTE**
3	**TABLESPOONS SOY SAUCE**
1	**TABLESPOON KOREAN SESAME OIL**
1	**POUND NOODLES**
2	**SCALLIONS, CRUSHED TO A PASTE IN A PROCESSOR**
4	**GARLIC CLOVES, CRUSHED TO A PASTE**

1 Cook the chicken in water or broth and salt until tender, about 45 minutes. Remove the chicken and reserve the broth. Shred the meat by hand; discard skin and bones. Mix the shreds with the chili powder, soy sauce and sesame oil. Mix well so that the chicken develops a red color.
2 Bring the reserved broth to a boil, add the noodles, scallion paste and garlic paste and cook until the noodles are *al dente*, about 5 minutes.
3 Pour the broth and noodles into a large serving bowl or individual bowls. Add the seasoned chicken to the center of the bowl but do not stir.

Serve warm.

Serves 6 or more.

Deulk Kae Kook

CHICKEN AND PERILLA SOUP

Traveling around Korea as I did doing research in the markets, I frequently noticed bundles of perilla leaves, also called wild sesame in Korea, or beefsteak plant (*P. frutescens*). The leaves are sliced and included in stir-fry dishes. It is the seeds that we are concerned with here; they are ground to a powder and included as one of the seasonings in the soup. The seeds, which are smaller and rounder than standard sesame seeds, provide a light tan color to the soup.

Koreans consider this soup a health food since it contains vegetables and poultry rather than red meat and is cooked without fat.

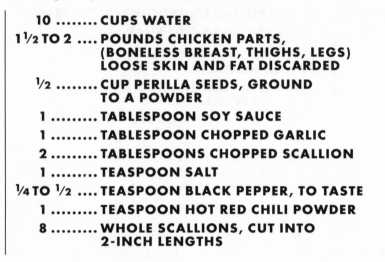

10	CUPS WATER
1½ TO 2	POUNDS CHICKEN PARTS, (BONELESS BREAST, THIGHS, LEGS) LOOSE SKIN AND FAT DISCARDED
½	CUP PERILLA SEEDS, GROUND TO A POWDER
1	TABLESPOON SOY SAUCE
1	TABLESPOON CHOPPED GARLIC
2	TABLESPOONS CHOPPED SCALLION
1	TEASPOON SALT
¼ TO ½	TEASPOON BLACK PEPPER, TO TASTE
1	TEASPOON HOT RED CHILI POWDER
8	WHOLE SCALLIONS, CUT INTO 2-INCH LENGTHS

1 Bring the water to a boil in a large pan, add the chicken parts, and cook over moderate heat for 1 hour. Remove the chicken from the broth and reserve the broth. Cool and separate the meat, discarding the skin and bones. Tear the meat into shreds.

2 Add the ground perilla seeds to the reserved broth, which has reduced somewhat; bring to a boil and cook over moderate heat for 15 minutes.

3 Add the seasonings to the chicken shreds—the soy sauce, garlic, chopped scallions, salt, pepper and chili powder—and mix well. Add the mixture to the broth and simmer over low heat for 15 minutes. Add the scallion lengths and cook for 5 minutes more.

Serve warm.

Serves 6.

VARIATION: *It may not be an easy task to locate the perilla seeds, so toasted sesame seeds may be substituted. Grind them into a powder and follow the instructions as noted.*

Tubu Jigae

Soybean curd is popular in Korea because of its high protein content and also because it can be steamed, boiled or fried to good effect. This soup features the firm or Chinese-type of curd in a fat-free, almost completely vegetarian soup, enriched with a small amount of beef-steak. Koreans serve soup along with the other dishes to lubricate the food as they dine.

1/4	POUND SIRLOIN STEAK, SLICED THIN
1	MEDIUM-SIZE ONION, PEELED, CUT INTO 1/4 INCH-THICK SLICES (1/2 CUP)
1	GARLIC CLOVE, CRUSHED
1	MEDIUM-SIZE POTATO, PEELED, CUT INTO 1/4-INCH SLICES
1	ZUCCHINI CUT INTO 3-INCH PIECE
2	DRIED MUSHROOMS, SOAKED IN WATER FOR 1 HOUR, DRAINED AND QUARTERED
3	CUPS WATER
2	SCALLIONS, CUT INTO 3-INCH PIECES
1	FIRM SOYBEAN CURD, CUT INTO 16 CUBES
1/2	TEASPOON SALT, OR TO TASTE
1/8	TEASPOON PEPPER
1	TEASPOON HOT RED CHILI POWDER
1	EGG, BEATEN

1 Stir-fry the steak in a saucepan without oil for 1/2 minute, just enough to change the color. Add the onion and garlic and stir-fry over moderate heat for 1/2 minute more.

2 Add the potato, zucchini, mushrooms and water. Cover the pan, bring to a boil and cook for 10 minutes. Then add the scallions, bean curd, salt, pepper and red chili powder and simmer for 10 minutes.

3 Dribble the egg in around the surface of the soup, cover the pan, and cook over low heat for 5 minutes more.

Serve warm with other dishes on the menu.

Serves 4.

Kongnamul Kook

SOYBEAN SPROUT SOUP

Most of the bean sprouts that one can see in Asian food shops are prepared from the small green mung bean. Also seen occasionally are larger sprouts with the 2 halves of the bean prominently attached to the stem. These are yellow soybeans, which have been germinated in the dark and which are used in the Kongnamul Kook.

½ ..... POUND YELLOW SOYBEAN SPROUTS

7 ...... CUPS COLD WATER

1 ...... TEASPOON SALT, OR TO TASTE

3 ...... SCALLIONS, CUT INTO 1-INCH LENGTHS

1 ...... TEASPOON CHOPPED GINGER

1 ...... TEASPOON TOASTED SESAME SEEDS

1 ...... TEASPOON KOREAN SESAME OIL

1 ...... TEASPOON HOT CHILI POWDER (GOCHU KARU)

1 ...... EGG, BEATEN (OPTIONAL BUT RECOMMENDED)

1 Prepare the bean sprouts by snipping off the root end and removing the bean skin which might still be attached to the sprout.

2 Bring the 7 cups cold water to a boil and add all the other ingredients except the beaten egg. Cook over moderate heat for 6 minutes, then reduce heat to low and simmer for 6 minutes more. (My teacher cautioned me not to uncover the pan during this time since it releases a "fishy" aroma.)

3 Dribble the egg, if used, into the boiling soup, remove from the heat and serve immediately.

Serve hot.

Serves 8 with other foods.

Daegoo Jiri

FRESH COD IN BROTH

Most people think of the cod as a fish of the northern waters of the United
States, Canada and the North Sea. This thick, white, firm-fleshed fish
is also found in northern Pacific waters around Korea and is equally
popular there. Koreans appreciate this fish especially in soups such
as this easily assembled Daegoo Jiri.

5 TO 6	CUPS WATER
1	TEASPOON SALT, OR TO TASTE
2	THIN SLICES OF FRESH GINGER
1/4	POUND KOREAN RADISH, CUT INTO 1-INCH CUBES
2	POUNDS FRESH COD, RINSED WELL IN COLD WATER, CUT INTO 8 PIECES
1/8	TEASPOON BLACK OR WHITE PEPPER
1	LARGE SCALLION, CUT INTO 2-INCH DIAGONAL LENGTHS
1 OR 2	SPRIGS OF WATERCRESS OR CHRYSANTHEMUM LEAVES

1 Bring the water to a boil in a large pan. Add the salt, ginger, radish
and cod and cook over moderate heat for 10 minutes. The fish should
be firm yet cooked through.
2 Now add the pepper and scallion and stir a moment.

Serve hot, garnished with watercress or chrysanthemum leaves.

Serves 4 to 6 with rice and an assortment of side dishes.

Nokdoo Juk

MUNG BEAN PORRIDGE

Mung beans have several different uses, not only to produce the universally appreciated bean sprouts, but also to make this porridge. Mung beans have a green jacket which must be removed before preparing the porridge. Soak them in water to cover for 4 hours. Rub the beans briskly between your palms, which will loosen the skins. Pour off soaking water and discard skins. It is the skinless yellow bean that is used. Dried skinless yellow beans can be purchased ready for use in Korean groceries.

The porridge is a special-time snack for adults, or is served to the sick or those who wish to renew their energy sources. It is both strengthening and palatable.

1 ...... CUP MUNG BEANS, SKINLESS

8 ...... CUPS WATER

1 ...... CUP STICKY RICE, SOAKED IN WATER FOR 2 HOURS, DRAINED

1 TO 2.... TEASPOONS SALT, OR TO TASTE

1 Put the mung beans and water in a large pan, bring to a boil, then cook over moderate heat for 1 hour, or until beans are quite soft. To test, squeeze several between thumb and forefinger to crush them. Pour the very soft beans and the liquid through a metal sieve and press everything through into a bowl. There should be 4 to 5 cups of puréed beans and bean liquid.

2 Put the sticky rice and salt into the bean liquid and simmer over low heat for about ½ hour, which is sufficient to reduce the rice to a porridge with some texture. Adjust the salt if needed.

Serve hot.

Serves 4 to 6.

Kongnamu Neng Kook

COLD AROMATIC BEAN-SPROUT SOUP

Several cultures, like the Indonesians, Burmese and Koreans, for example, trim the head and tail of a bean sprout for aesthetic reasons. It is a strange sight to see the household cook trimming the sprouts, with a neat pile of pinched-off pieces in a heap on the table, but the sprouts do look better and do cook more uniformly. You may wish to follow their example for this summer soup.

½...... **POUND OF FRESH BEAN SPROUTS, WELL RINSED IN COLD WATER**
1 ...... **SCALLION, SLICED THIN**
3 ...... **GARLIC CLOVES, SLICED VERY THIN**
1 ...... **THIN SLICE OF FRESH GINGER, CRUSHED**
1 ...... **TEASPOON WHITE VINEGAR**
½...... **TEASPOON SUGAR**
5 ...... **DRIED HOT RED CHILI THREADS**
2 ...... **CUPS COLD WATER**

1 Blanch the bean sprouts in lightly salted boiling water and let stand for 2 minutes. Drain and cool.
2 Toss the sprouts with the scallion, garlic, ginger, vinegar, sugar and chili threads. Put the mixture into a serving bowl and pour the 2 cups cold water over. Mix well.

Serve in individual bowls.

Serves 4.

Naeng Kook

SUMMER SEAWEED SOUP

Part of the charm of Cheju, the unbelievably picturesque island, is that the food differs somewhat from mainland Korea. As well as the incessant wind, the rock formations and offshore islets that dot the horizon, the food, too, has developed its own character. This altogether satisfying summer soup is clear and cold and has a light flavor of the vinegar, tempered delicately with sugar.

6 TO 8 ...	**PIECES OF DRIED SEAWEED**
2	**CUPS COLD WATER**
¼......	**TEASPOON SUGAR**
½......	**TEASPOON WHITE OR CIDER VINEGAR**
¼......	**CUP JULIENNE STRIPS OF KOREAN RADISH**
¼......	**CUP JULIENNE STRIPS OF YOUNG CUCUMBER**
1	**TABLESPOON JULIENNE STRIPS OF CARROT**

1 Rinse the seaweed thoroughly to remove any sand lurking in the folds. Soak in water for 20 minutes; drain and rinse.
2 Mix the seaweed with the cold water, sugar, vinegar, radish, cucumber and carrot. Adjust the amount of sugar and vinegar, if you desire.

Serve cold.

Serves 2 or 3.

Naeng Myon

COLD NOODLE SOUP

It was on a very hot midday in Kyongju that I first tasted this soup. The
cool, beef-flavored, completely fat-free broth was filled with a round
mound of buckwheat noodles, which my waitress cut into halves with
scissors at the table to simplify eating. This popular soup made a complete meal on a hot day in southeast Korea.

2 ...... POUNDS BONELESS BEEF CHUCK
PLUS 1/2 POUND BEEF BONES

12 ..... CUPS WATER

2 ...... INCHES OF FRESH GINGER,
PEELED AND SLICED

1 ...... TEASPOON SALT

1/2 ...... POUND BUCKWHEAT NOODLES

Garnishes

1 ...... KIRBY CUCUMBER, ENDS TRIMMED,
RINSED IN LIGHTLY SALTED WATER,
CUT INTO JULIENNE

1/4 ...... WHITE KOREAN RADISH, PEELED,
CUT INTO JULIENNE

1 ...... SEMI-HOT GREEN CHILI, HALVED
LENGTHWISE, SEEDED, SLICED
THIN DIAGONALLY

1 ...... TEASPOON SALT

1/2 ...... TEASPOON WHITE OR CIDER VINEGAR

1/2 ...... TEASPOON TOASTED SESAME SEEDS

2 ...... TABLESPOONS DRY MUSTARD MIXED
WITH 2 TABLESPOONS COLD WATER

tagedi (pepper) sauce

1 ...... TEASPOON PEPPER

1 ...... TEASPOON KOREAN SESAME OIL

1 ..... GARLIC CLOVE CRUSHED TO A PASTE

1/4 ...... TEASPOON SALT

3 ...... HARD-COOKED EGGS, HALVED

1 To prepare the soup, put the beef, water, ginger and salt in a
pan large enough to contain all the ingredients, bring to a boil, and

(Continued next page)

remove the dark foam. Cook slowly over low heat for 2 hours. Remove the beef, which is now tender, and refrigerate. Discard the ginger. When the soup is finally cooked it should have about 12 cups broth. During the cooking process the liquid will evaporate so one must probably add another cup water.

Refrigerate the broth overnight to congeal the accumulated fat. Discard the hardened fat. You now have a clear, seasoned, cold broth. Cut the beef into paper-thin slices.

2 Bring about 5 cups water to a boil in a pan, add the noodles without breaking them, and cook over moderate heat for 2 minutes. The noodles should be *al dente*. Drain and rinse under cold water.

3 To prepare the garnishes, put the cucumber, radish, chili and salt in a bowl. Toss well to mix and let stand for 10 minutes. Then rinse in cold water, drain, and toss with the vinegar and sesame seeds. Set aside.

4 Mix the mustard and water and mix together the ingredients for the tagedi pepper sauce. Serve the 2 sauces on small plates with the soup. Each diner will help himself to as much as he wants to mix with the soup or to season the beef slices.

5 Divide the noodles into 6 portions and put a portion into each soup bowl. Pour 2 cups cold broth over the noodles and spread a garnish assortment over the top. Place half of a hard-cooked egg in the center and add a portion of beef slices.

Serve the soup cold.

Serves 6.

Pot

RED BEAN PORRIDGE

The red beans used here are the Asian variety—those we call soybeans.
The *pot* is prepared and served when the severe winters settle down
over the Korean peninsula, especially in the northern regions. There
are two versions of the bean porridge, the salty type which also contains sticky rice and the sweet-snack type which does not. Both are
thick, smooth porridges and usually kept for special occasions.

1 ...... **CUP RED SOYBEANS, NOT SOAKED**
8 ...... **CUPS WATER**
1 ...... **CUP STICKY RICE, WELL RINSED IN
COLD WATER**
1 TO 2.... **TEASPOONS SALT, OR TO TASTE**

1 Put the beans and water in a large pan and bring to a boil. Lower
the heat and simmer for about 2 hours or until the beans are soft
enough to be crushed between thumb and forefinger. Strain the mixture through a metal sieve and rub through into a bowl. Discard the
skins that remain in the sieve.
2 Add the rice and salt to the bean purée and liquid. Simmer over
low heat for about $1/2$ hour, or until the rice has a quite soft, porridge texture. Adjust the salt if necessary.

Serves 4 to 6 .

VARIATION: Dan Pot Juk *(Sweet Red Bean Porridge): Prepare 1 recipe Red Bean
Porridge without the rice and salt. Add 2 tablespoons sugar and simmer over low heat
for 10 minutes. Serve as a snack.*

Jat Juk

CREAM OF PINE NUT PORRIDGE

What an extraordinary porridge—subtle, refined and with a smooth, creamy consistency. It is the only one of its kind in Asian cooking and probably in the rest of the world as well. The Jat Juk is so unlike the other vividly seasoned dishes of Korea that it must be given a place of its own. The porridge, it is not quite a soup, is usually served on three different occasions. The first is for breakfast as a special treat, since pine nuts are expensive everywhere. The second is as a restorer of strength for persons who are ill or debilitated. The third occasion is as a snack anytime of day when special friends meet—not the tea or coffee hour but pine-nut soup time.

- $1/2$ ...... CUP PINE NUTS
- 1 ...... CUP WATER
- 4 ...... DRIED JUJUBES (KOREAN DATES), SOAKED IN WATER FOR 2 HOURS
- 2 ...... TEASPOONS HONEY
- $1/4$ ...... CUP RICE FLOUR DISSOLVED IN $1/2$ CUP WATER, LEFT FOR 5 MINUTES
- $1/4$ ...... TEASPOON SUGAR
- $1/8$ ...... TEASPOON SALT

1 Grind the pine nuts in a processor with $1/2$ cup of the water for about $1/2$ minute. Add the balance of the water and process the mixture until smooth. Pour through a metal strainer and rub the particles through, preferably with a wooden spoon. Discard the small amount of residue, which is mostly the "eyes" or buds of the pine nuts.

2 When the jujubes are ready, cut out and discard the pits. Cut the jujubes into thin slices and mix with the honey. Set aside.

3 Simmer the rice flour paste in a pan over low heat, stirring constantly with a wooden spoon until the mixture just starts to bubble. This is the soup thickener.

4 Add the pine nut mixture, the sugar and salt to the rice flour and bring to a low boil for 2 minutes. The lightly thickened porridge, smooth and creamy, is now ready.

Pour it into individual bowls and garnish with a teaspoon of the jujube and honey.

Serve warm.

Serves 4.

Rice and Noodles

It was during August, a month of heavy rains in the southwestern part of Korea where much of the rice is grown, and I was driving through the countryside as a deluge struck the incomparably green rice paddies stretching in all directions. Nurtured by so much water and a fertile soil, no green could have been greener than the rice fields of Korea as I saw them that day. The vista was broken here and there by an occasional farmhouse with its large black pottery storage jars on the rooftop, silhouetted against the sky.

Rice is not only the main crop but the staff of life for Koreans in this area; the medium-grain sticky rice is used almost exclusively. When cooked it has a soft and somewhat melting consistency but it does not congeal into an amorphous mass. The grains of rice when cooked are still shiny and retain their individual shape. It is an admirable foil for the sometimes overpowering strength of the hot chili and dilutes the intensity of the flavors. Rice itself is cooked plain rather than extravagantly seasoned like the fried rices of China, Indonesia and other countries. It is sometimes supplemented by combining it with barley, which has been grown in Korea since ancient times, or with white, red or black soybeans or chestnuts in token quantities for protein. Rice prepared the Korean way is not fattening as evidenced by the slim figures of the people who sometimes have rice 2 or 3 times a day. A very few recipes do call for glutinous rice when its special sweetness is needed. But the principal ingredient is the cooked white rice.

Noodles are second only to rice in importance and once were considered the poor man's food for those families who could not afford rice. The buckwheat noodle, for example, is North Korean in origin and still highly valued in that section. The Korean word *kalgo-oksu* means knife-cut noodles since they were prepared in the homes—mixed, rolled out on a flat surface and handcut into strips. The noodles were therefore flat. Now we have round noodles, machine-made and spewed out through round discs.

Today, hand cut or commercially made, noodles are no longer second-class but hold their own in the Korean cuisine.

Bap

Koreans use a medium-grain sticky rice almost exclusively, but long grain or glutinous rice may be cooked in these proportions, if preferred.

**1 .... CUP RICE, WELL RINSED IN COLD
            WATER, DRAINED**

1²/₃ .... CUPS WATER

1 Put the rice and water into a pan and bring to a boil. Reduce the heat to low, cover the pan, and simmer for about 12 minutes. Stir the rice once toward the end of that time. If it appears to be dry and still hard, I add 1 or 2 tablespoons water and cook for another minute or two.
2 Turn off the heat and let the rice stand for 10 minutes more. The heat will steam the rice to completion.

Serve warm.

Makes 3 cups.

Bibimbap

RICE MEDLEY IN A CLAY POT

The provincial capital of Chonju is famous in the rest of Korea for this Bibimbap, which is rice with all the fixings. The custom is to serve individual Bibimbaps in the black clay pots known as *tukbaege*, which can be placed directly over a flame or heating element.

It was in a well-known restaurant in Chonju that I ate my first Bibimbap, one filled with sticky rice and sprinkled with a generous number of laver (seaweed) shreds.

Separately, on a dinner plate, were arranged small mounds of bean sprouts, slices of beefsteak, a fried egg, gochu jang (hot chili paste), sliced scallions, toasted sesame seeds and some Korean sesame oil. The diner can see exactly what he is getting. I slipped all the ingredients from the plate into the hot pot and mixed them together with a pair of nicely tapered stainless-steel chopsticks. The pot remained warm for the entire meal.

Side dishes were a salty puréed anchovy paste, eggplant Muchim, Korean radish with its own sweet fermented flavor and several thin strands of carrot and a floating whole green semi-hot chili, fiery red Cabbage Kimchi and a scallion sauté — each a side dish with a different impact. The name of the game is quantity, quality and variety. Here is the recipe.

	CORN OIL FOR THE CLAY POT OR A COVERED SKILLET
1½	CUPS COOKED RICE (SEE P. 149)
2	HEAPING TABLESPOONS JULIENNE STRIPS OF BEEFSTEAK, STIR-FRIED IN 1 TEASPOON OIL FOR 1 MINUTE
1 TO 2	TEASPOONS GOCHU JANG, TO TASTE
¼	CUP BEAN SPROUTS, BLANCHED IN BOILING WATER FOR 2 MINUTES, DRAINED WELL
1	SCALLION, SLICED THIN
2	HEAPING TABLESPOONS JULIENNED YOUNG CUCUMBER
2	TABLESPOONS SHREDDED LAVER
1	FRIED EGG, SUNNYSIDE UP
1	TEASPOON KOREAN SESAME OIL

1 Rub the clay pot (*tukbaege*) or a metal pan with corn oil on the bottom and sides. Add the rice, cover and warm over moderate heat for 3 minutes.

2 Then place all the ingredients on the rice in the order listed, with the fried egg on top, spooning the sesame oil over all. Serve at once. The diners may mix everything together at the table, or in a more modern vein, the Bibimbap can be mixed in the kitchen and served in a bowl. But the traditional way is more attractive.

Serve warm.

Serves 2 Americans or 1 Korean (who will prefer 2 teaspoons of the gochu jang).

Chungmun *Bibimbap*

I tasted this Bibimbap in several restaurants around Korea. It is made with rice and anything from a simple vegetarian combination to one with beef and shellfish, and is served in the clay pot known as a *tukbaege*. This particular recipe, the finest Bibimbap I had, was served to me at the Chungmun Golf Club (an unlikely location) on Cheju Island. It was a masterpiece from the hands of a fine cook.

1	CUP COOKED RICE
1	TEASPOON KOREAN SESAME OIL
1	LIGHTLY FRIED EGG, SUNNYSIDE UP
¼	CUP BEAN SPROUTS, BLANCHED IN BOILING WATER FOR 1 MINUTE, DRAINED AND PRESSED FIRMLY TO ELIMINATE WATER
3	SLICES OF ZUCCHINI, CUT INTO JULIENNE STRIPS
3	GREEN BEANS, SLICED THIN DIAGONALLY, BLANCHED IN BOILING WATER FOR 2 MINUTES, DRAINED WELL
2	DRIED MUSHROOMS, SOAKED IN WATER FOR 1 HOUR, DRAINED AND CUT INTO JULIENNE STRIPS
3	SLICES OF CARROT, CUT INTO JULIENNE STRIPS
2	OUNCES BEEFSTEAK, CUT INTO 1-INCH JULIENNE STRIPS, STIR-FRIED IN 1 TEASPOON CORN OIL FOR 1 MINUTE
6	THIN SLICES OF SMOKED SALMON, CUT INTO 1-INCH SQUARES
2	OUNCES COOKED SQUID, CUT INTO 1-INCH STRIPS
1	SCALLION, SLICED THIN
1	OUNCE JULIENNE SLIVERS OF ABALONE OR CLAM MEAT
2	TABLESPOONS GOCHU JANG

Mix the rice and sesame oil together and put it into a flameproof clay pot or skillet with a cover. Put the egg on top of the heap, pushing the rice around to conceal the white but not the yolk, which is the center decorative object. Place all the other ingredients in orderly piles around the top and sides of the pot. Cover and put directly on the gas or electric unit of the stove over moderate heat. Heat for 3 minutes until the rice sizzles and all the ingredients are heated through. Remove the cover so that the diners may admire the variety of ingredients, then mix everything together and serve.

Serves 2.

NOTE: *The Bibimbap is sometimes mixed together in the kitchen but this conceals the variety of the ingredients. Serving it in individual heaps informs the diner of the extent to which the cook has gone to include rich or expensive ingredients. One can reduce the number of vegetables and seafood but a large variety ensures more interesting dining.*

Nokdoo Ciru Pyun

STEAMED RICE CAKE WITH MUNG BEANS

Glutinous rice, also known as sweet rice, is reserved in Asia for special occasions, many times for sweets. The rice is dense and gummy and can be attractive to western tastes. The Nokdoo has simple ingredients, is vegetarian, fat-free and delicious, if unconventional, for the tea and coffee hour snack.

3 ...... **CUPS GLUTINOUS RICE**
2 ...... **CUPS SKINLESS YELLOW MUNG BEANS**
2 ...... **TEASPOONS SALT**
¼ ...... **CUP SUGAR**

1 Rinse the rice well, cover with cold water and soak overnight or for 12 hours. Drain well and grind in a processor. This will result in a dense, sticky paste.

2 Cover the beans well with cold water and soak for 2 hours. Drain. Put the beans in a Chinese-style steamer and steam them for 15 minutes. Grind the beans coarsely in a processor. Mix them with the salt and sugar.

3 Wrap a wet kitchen towel (flat, not Turkish weave) over and around the perforated steamer tray. Prepare a layered cake on the towel in this way: Put down in a round or rectangular shape a layer ¼ inch thick of the ground mung beans. Cover this with ½ inch of the glutinous rice and cover with another ¼ inch of the beans. Cover the steamer tightly and steam for 45 minutes to 1 hour. Test with a toothpick. If the toothpick emerges dry, then the cake is done.

4 Lift out the cake in the towel and carefully turn it upside down on a cutting board. Allow the cake to cool somewhat and slice into convenient sections while still warm. Serve immediately while fresh with tea or coffee.

The cake should be stored in a freezer since it does ferment when refrigerated for more than 1 day. Put the cake sections in aluminum or plastic trays, cover and freeze. Remove when wanted and rewarm in a steamer for 5 to 10 minutes.

NOTE: *The green skinned mung beans are used to sprout the standard bean sprouts. The skinless yellow mung beans used for this cake can be purchased in Korean groceries.*
If the skinless yellow mung beans are unavailable, you may use the green mung beans but they must be skinned before preparing the rice cake. Soak them in water to cover for 4 hours. Rub the beans between your hands in the water and the skins will separate quite easily. Drain, discard the skins, and use the green beans as noted in the recipe except that additional soaking is not necessary.

Bam Baap

CHESTNUT RICE

Korean chestnuts are the size of a small egg—very large, solid and sweet.
It is astonishing in the autumn, the chestnut season, to see a large
heap of these giant chestnuts piled in pyramids in the public market-
places. In New York, during the Thanksgiving/Christmas season,
reasonably good chestnuts imported from Italy are available and
make a satisfactory substitute.

2 ...... CUPS RICE
6 ...... CHESTNUTS (SEE NOTE)
3¹/₂ ..... CUPS WATER

1 Rinse the rice in cold water and drain.
2 Peel the chestnuts of their outer brown skins and the inner, thin-
ner skin linings. Cut them into halves, if large, or leave them
whole if they are small.
3 Combine the rice, chestnuts and water, bring to a boil, then
reduce heat to low and cook for about 15 minutes. Stir once or twice
toward the end of the cooking. The water will have been absorbed
and the chestnuts softened.

Serve warm.

Serves 6 at Korean meals.

NOTE: *I prepare the chestnuts in this manner: Chestnuts that have been well dried by
leaving them at room temperature for a day or two are easier to peel with a serrated knife.
Sometimes the peel can be broken off with your fingers. To remove the inner and outer skin,
I cut off about half of the thick outer shell and drop the chestnuts in boiling water. Cover
the pan and cook for 5 minutes. Drain, cool enough to handle, then pull off both skins.*

O Kok

5-GRAIN RICE

This is a festive combination of beans with 5 different grains including the glutinous (sweet) rice with its dense, viscous texture and lightly sweet flavor. Glutinous rice is not usually cooked alone but in combination with other grains. It requires less liquid in cooking than standard sticky or long-grain rices. The 5-grain combination is recommended for diabetics since it is not acidic.

2	**CUPS GLUTINOUS RICE**
¼	**CUP BARLEY**
½	**CUP GREEN AND/OR YELLOW MILLET, EQUAL AMOUNTS MIXED TOGETHER**
¼	**CUP SORGHUM (SUSU), RED-GRAINED VARIETY**
½	**CUP RED SOYBEANS**
¾	**TEASPOON SALT**

1 Cover the glutinous rice with water and soak overnight. Drain.
2 In another pan, soak the barley, green and yellow millet and the sorghum grains overnight, covered with water. Then drain.
3 Cook the red beans slowly in about 4 cups water. The beans are quite hard and will take from 2 to 3 hours of cooking. Then test a bean by squeezing to see if it can be crushed. If so, the beans are ready. Reserve the liquid and measure it. Add enough water to make a total of $2\frac{1}{2}$ cups liquid. Set aside.
4 Mix the glutinous rice, red beans, barley, millet, sorghum and salt all together, add the reserved bean liquid, and bring to a boil. Reduce heat to very low and cook for about 12 minutes, enough to soften all the ingredients. The liquid from the red beans will tint the 5 grains a pink color.

Serve warm or at room temperature.

Serves 6 to 8.

Pat Baap

The Asian red bean is not the American variety (red kidney beans) but arose independently on a different continent, and is what we know as the red soybean. It is quite hard and must be cooked before combining with the sticky rice. Should you mix the beans and their cooking liquid with the rice, the mixture will be tinted pink, which I prefer. Some cooks pour off the bean liquid and just add the softened beans to the rice to result in a white mixture. It is a matter of choice.

$\frac{1}{2}$ ..... CUP RED BEANS, WELL RINSED
3 ...... CUPS WATER
2 ...... CUPS RICE, WELL RINSED
$\frac{1}{2}$ ..... TEASPOON SALT

1 Bring the beans and water to a boil in a pan over moderate heat, reduce heat to low and cook, partially covered, for about 1 hour, or long enough to soften the beans. Squeeze a bean in your fingers to test readiness.

2 Drain the beans and reserve the liquid. Add enough water to the bean liquid to have a total of $3\frac{3}{4}$ cups. Mix the liquid, beans, rice and salt together and bring to a boil. Reduce heat to low, cover the pan, and cook for about 15 minutes. This should be enough to soften the rice and beans.

Serve warm.

Serves 6 with traditional Korean dishes.

Jap Chae

VEGETABLE, NOODLE AND STEAK STIR-FRY

One of the more popular Korean dishes is Jap Chae. Using familiar ingredients with a variety of textures, colors, flavors and simple seasonings, the mixture can be prepared for any number of guests or family. It lends itself to preparation in generous quantities as well as variations in the choice of vegetables.

3 ...... OUNCES KOREAN VERMICELLI (SEE NOTE)
3 ...... TABLESPOONS CORN OIL
1 .... LARGE ONION, CHOPPED COARSELY (1 CUP)
½ ...... POUND FLANK OR SIRLOIN STEAK, SLICED INTO STRIPS 3 INCHES LONG AND 1 INCH WIDE
1 ...... CARROT, CUT INTO 3-INCH JULIENNE STRIPS (¾ CUP)
1 ...... SMALL GREEN PEPPER, SEEDED, CUT INTO 3-INCH JULIENNE STRIPS (1 CUP)
½ ..... POUND CHINESE CHIVES, WELL-RINSED, CUT INTO 3-INCH LENGTHS, OR ½ POUND FRESH SPINACH, WELL RINSED, STEMS TRIMMED
½ ..... TEASPOON SALT
2 ...... TEASPOONS SUGAR
1 ...... TABLESPOON SOY SAUCE
1 ...... TEASPOON KOREAN SESAME OIL
¼ ...... CUP TREE EARS, SOAKED IN WARM WATER FOR ½ HOUR, DRAINED, RINSED WELL

1 Bring 4 cups water to a boil in a large pan. Add the vermicelli and boil over moderate heat for 3 minutes. This is enough to soften the noodles but still retain some texture. Do not overcook. Drain in a metal sieve and rinse under cold water; drain well and set aside. The noodles are translucent when cooked but still firm.
2 Heat the oil in a wok, add the onion, and stir-fry over moderate heat for 2 minutes. Add the beef and continue to fry for 1 minute. Now add the carrot, green pepper, chives or spinach as you stir-fry for 2 minutes more.
3 Add the salt, sugar, soy sauce, sesame oil and tree ears. Stir-fry and toss the mixture for a minute. Lastly, fold in the vermicelli and mix well.

Serve warm.

Serves 4 with salads and kimchi.

NOTE: *Korean vermicelli is prepared from sweet potato and cornstarch and is grayish in color with a stiff consistency. I use the Dang Myun brand but there are others.*

Bibim Naeng Myon

Buckwheat is not a common cereal. Its black, triangular seeds are ground into flour and made into a very thin, dry, tan-colored vermicelli that has a somewhat sticky consistency when cooked. It is this vermicelli that is used in this cold noodle salad, enriched artfully with substantial flavors and textures. It is especially liked in North Korea.

Although there are a number of steps in the preparation of this salad, everything may be done in advance and refrigerated.

Noodles

- 1 ...... **PACKAGE DRY BUCKWHEAT NOODLES (1 1/2 POUNDS)**
- 2 ...... **TABLESPOONS KOREAN SESAME OIL**
- 1/2 ..... **TEASPOON SALT**

Beef Garnish

- 3/4 ..... **POUND FLANK OR SIRLOIN STEAK, SHREDDED INTO 2-INCH LENGTHS**
- 1 1/2 .... **TABLESPOONS SOY SAUCE**
- 2 ...... **TEASPOONS SUGAR**
- 1 ...... **TABLESPOON CHOPPED SCALLION, GREEN PART ONLY**
- 1 ...... **GARLIC CLOVE, CHOPPED**
- 1/4 ..... **TEASPOON BLACK PEPPER**
- 1 ...... **TEASPOON KOREAN SESAME OIL**

Vegetable Garnish

- 1 ...... **HARD CRISP CHINESE OR KOREAN PEAR**
- 2 ...... **KIRBY CUCUMBERS, HALVED LENGTHWISE, THEN SLICED DIAGONALLY, MIXED WITH 1/2 TEASPOON SALT FOR 10 MINUTES, DRIED**
- 2 ...... **EGGS, SEPARATED**
- 1/2 ..... **POUND KOREAN RADISH, PEELED, SHREDDED, MIXED WITH 1/2 TEASPOON SALT FOR 10 MINUTES, THEN LIQUID SQUEEZED OUT**
- 1/2 ..... **TEASPOON HOT RED CHILI POWDER**
- 1/2 ..... **TEASPOON WHITE OR CIDER VINEGAR**
- 1 ...... **TEASPOON SUGAR**

(Continued next page)

4......GARLIC CLOVES, CHOPPED FINE

2......TABLESPOONS GOCHU JANG PASTE

2......TABLESPOONS SUGAR

2......TEASPOONS KOREAN SESAME OIL

1......TABLESPOON TOASTED SESAME SEEDS

1 Bring 10 cups water to a boil over high heat in a large pan, add the noodles, cover the pan, and cook until the foam rises and moves the cover. Uncover, let the foam subside, cover again, and repeat the boiling and foaming a total of 3 times. Drain and run cold water over the noodles to remove the starch. Do not break the long strands during the cooking and draining processes. The salad should have long, *al dente* noodles.

2 Now mix in the sesame oil and salt, which prevents the noodles from sticking together. Refrigerate for future use or set aside if you intend to complete the recipe.

3 Put all the beef garnish ingredients into a skillet and stir-fry over moderate heat for 2 minutes. Set aside.

4 Peel the pear and cut into 2- to 3-inch-long julienne strips.

5 Put the cucumber slices into a nonstick pan and stir-fry over high heat for 10 seconds, which will bring out a strong green color to the skin.

6 Prepare 2 omelets—one with the egg whites and one with the yolks.

7 Thoroughly mix the radish with the chili powder, vinegar and sugar. Set aside.

8 Combine all the seasoning ingredients into a paste.

9 When ready to serve, put the noodles in a large serving dish or bowl. Arrange groups of the vegetable garnish over the noodles, independently of each other in separate piles, such as the pear, cucumber, omelets and radish.

10 The seasoned beef garnish and the seasoning paste are served separately in their own bowls. Each diner takes the noodles and whatever he wishes of the vegetables, seasoned beef, and seasoning paste to taste. Then everything is tossed together by the diner. Or the noodles and other ingredients may be put into one large bowl and tossed together in the kitchen.

Serve at room temperature.

Serves 6 to 8.

*F*ish and *S*eafood

Korea is married to the sea. Nowhere on the peninsula can one be unaware of the seas' influence—on weather, occupation, recreation and certainly on the food; it is only to be expected that seafood is the most popular category of their cuisine. Seafood is available in the finest quality and in great quantity and variety, is inexpensive and a highly important source of protein for the entire population. Using Korean seasonings, the cooks have created an endless variety of mouthwatering concoctions.

A walking investigation of the great public fish market in the southern city of Pusan is a lesson in the varieties that have been pulled from the seas, with a half mile of one pristine seafood stall after another, featuring the specialty of each fishmonger: oysters, clams, mussels—in and out of their shells; or fish of all sizes and shapes—some familiar, others unknown—but all with eager buyers. Meticulously organized, immaculately clean and with the fresh aroma of the sea blowing in from the harbor, this market is an ichthyological exhibition presented for a population with a mania for freshness, health and cleanliness.

The East Sea teems with the ever-popular squid in the deep waters around the fabled Ullung Island. There one can see miles of squid drying in the sun during the fishing season, when about 9,000 tons are brought in by the fishermen. The muddy, tidal flats of the West Sea are home to millions of crabs, which are easily caught in the shallow waters and later will be served up in such preparations as Gye Tang, a crab stew.

In a society with a well-entrenched work ethic, energy pulses in every facet of the fishing industry. While the men are out in their boats fishing, it is the women who make up the sales force in the stalls of the retail markets and who prepare the seafood at home.

As with other aspects of Korean cooking, seafood, with its lack of fat and calories, fits right in with today's cooking philosophy.

A Fish Story

One day as I was cooking with a gentle and aristocratic Korean lady, she
began reminiscing about her childhood on a rather large estate in
Korea. One of the stories she told was this bizarre, perhaps diabolical, tale of the original method of preparing mudfish.

A rather muddy river ran through the grounds of her estate
and there lived a kind of loach or minnow, mudfish (*Misgurnus
anguillocaudatus*), called *mikuraj* or *chueu* in Korea. They were
small, dark, pencil-shaped fish, 3 to 4 inches long, commonly found
in the muddy water along the banks of many Korean rivers.

When these fish are caught they are put into brine which forces
them to spew out the mud, revealing a shiny, clean fish. Now they are
ready for cooking.

The cook pours a teaspoon or two of oil in a large skillet and
then places large squares of thick, creamy, homemade soybean curd
around the edge of the skillet, leaving the center open. (This is the
diabolical part.)

The skillet is heated and the live, clean fish are put into the pan.
When the fish feel the heat they try to escape, slithering around the
pan and wriggling into the squares or chunks of tubu for refuge, in
effect, stuffing it.

The stuffed tubu is used sliced and cooked in a denjang-flavored
soup—a dish considered a great delicacy by some.

Aw Jook

FISH AND RICE GRUEL

Chun Chon is a provincial capital in the interior of the eastern province of Korea. It has no access to the sea and so has turned to the rivers nearby for its supply of fish. The city is known for this rice gruel, a specialty of most restaurants. Aw Jook is noted for its concentrated flavor and also for the value of its healthful ingredients. It is a soup of health guaranteed to restore lost or misplaced energies.

6 OR 7 .... CUPS OF WATER

2 .... INCHES OF FRESH GINGER, SLICED

1½ TO 2... POUNDS OF ANY FRESHWATER FISH SUCH AS PERCH, CARP, WHITEFISH, USE THE WHOLE FISH WITH HEAD AND TAIL INTACT

¼ .... CUP RICE, WELL RINSED

Condiment

2 .... TABLESPOONS SOY SAUCE

3 .... TABLESPOONS CHOPPED SCALLIONS

1 TO 2 ...... TEASPOONS MINCED AND SEEDED FRESH HOT RED CHILI

1 .... TABLESPOON CHOPPED GARLIC

1 .... TEASPOON CHOPPED GINGER

1 .... TEASPOON KOREAN SESAME OIL

1 .... TABLESPOON TOASTED SESAME SEEDS

1 Bring the water to a boil; add the ginger and fish. Simmer in a covered pan over very low heat for 5 hours. All of the flavor will be extracted from the fish and ginger and some water will have evaporated. At the end of this time, strain the broth and press out the liquid from the fish with the flat of a spoon. Discard fish and ginger.

2 Add the rice to the broth and simmer over low heat for 1½ hours to reduce the mixture to a gruel. Set aside.

3 Mix the condiment ingredients together and use to season the gruel, to taste.

Serve the gruel warm with the extra condiment on the side.

Serves 4.

Chun Pochuk

ABALONE AND RICE STEW

The people of Cheju Island off the southern coast of Korea refer to this
preparation as abalone soup but the rice makes it more of a thick
stew or porridge in our terms. The famous Haenyo women divers
pull the abalone off ocean rocks where they are attached with powerful suckers. They then scoop out the flesh and sell it, keeping the
beautiful shell with its iridescent mother-of-pearl colors to sell
separately. I was able to collect a number of small abalone shells,
beachcombing in an isolated spot.

1 ...... CUP RICE, WELL RINSED
2 ...... TEASPOONS KOREAN SESAME OIL
¼ ...... CUP DICED FRESH ABALONE (SEE NOTE)
2 ...... CUPS WATER
¼ ...... TEASPOON SALT
2 ...... TEASPOONS TOASTED SESAME SEEDS

1 Put the rice and sesame oil in a skillet or pan and stir-fry over low
heat for about 3 minutes to toast the rice lightly.
2 Add the abalone, water and salt, bring to a boil, then cook over low
heat, covered, for 20 minutes.

Serve warm, garnished with the sesame seeds.

Serves 2.

NOTE: *Canned abalone, which may be the only type available, is acceptable. First
toast the rice in the sesame oil as indicated, add water and salt, and simmer over low
heat for 10 minutes. Add the abalone and 3 tablespoons of the thick liquid from the
can, which will heighten the flavor. Simmer for 10 minutes more.*

Saengsun Kooee

This is the simplest and most traditional fare of a people who are surrounded by seas that are prodigal in providing the finest of fish and seafood. The fish, fresh and flapping from the sea, do not require any embellishment. All the supplementary flavors are provided by side dishes of kimchi, salads, plain boiled white rice—and an appetite.

Mackerel, swordfish, bluefish, kingfish, salmon or similar fish that are dark fleshed and have natural oil are the tastiest.

1 TO 1½... POUNDS SALTWATER FISH
1 .... TEASPOON SALT
CORN OIL FOR BRUSHING THE CHARCOAL, GAS OR ELECTRIC GRILL

1 If a whole fish such as mackerel is used, remove the head and tail. Cut the fish into 4 equal pieces. Whatever fish you use, score the pieces several times on both sides. Sprinkle both sides with the salt and let stand for 15 minutes.
2 Heat the grill and brush with the oil, using a pastry brush. Place the fish pieces on the grill and cook for about 3 minutes on each side. Remove the pieces to a serving platter that has been lined with red or green lettuce leaves, sliced tomatoes and cucumbers.

Serves 4.

Saengsun Gui

BROILED FISH WITH A SAUCE

Broiling fish over wood fires is the old-fashioned method of cooking it
and the results cannot be faulted. Nowadays, especially in a mountainous country like Korea, where the hills have been stripped of trees to
provide charcoal, firewood has become an endangered species and so
gas and electric broilers are more apt to be used.

1 TO 1½	**POUNDS WHOLE FLOUNDER, CORVINA OR OTHER WHITE-FLESHED FISH**
1	**TEASPOON SALT**
2	**TABLESPOONS SOY SAUCE**
½	**TEASPOON SUGAR**
¼	**TEASPOON HOT RED CHILI POWDER**
1	**SCALLION, SLICED THIN**
½	**TEASPOON KOREAN SESAME OIL**
1	**TEASPOON TOASTED SESAME SEEDS**

1 Clean the fish, leaving the head and tail intact. For the flounder,
score the fish 4 times diagonally on the white side. Other types of
fish can be scored on either side. Sprinkle the salt into the incisions
and over the rest of the fish. Broil over gas, electric or charcoal for
about 3 minutes on each side. Remove to a serving platter.
2 Prepare the sauce. Mix together well the soy sauce, sugar, chili
powder, scallion, sesame oil and seeds. Pour this over the side of the
fish that has been scored and into the openings.

Serve warm with rice and salads.

Serves 4.

Sen Saen Yang Jung Chang Kui

GRILLED SPICED FISH

My first experience with this recipe was in the city of Chonju where I was served a mackerel in its freshest state. It had been grilled over charcoal and was served at room temperature with 16 side dishes. Outside the restaurant a violent rainstorm raged, then stopped as quickly as it had begun. It all seemed like a drama arranged for foreign guests, and part of the dining ambience.

The toasted sesame seeds and the marinating sauce formed a light crust and the aroma of smoke permeated the entire fish.

1 ...... **WHOLE SALTWATER FISH, ABOUT 1 POUND, RED SNAPPER, PORGY, FLOUNDER OR MACKEREL, GILLS REMOVED**

1 ...... **TEASPOON SALT**

2 ...... **TABLESPOONS CORN OIL**

1 ...... **TABLESPOON SOY SAUCE**

½...... **TEASPOON HOT RED CHILI POWDER**

1 ...... **GARLIC CLOVE, CHOPPED FINE**
PINCH OF BLACK PEPPER

1 ...... **TEASPOON TOASTED SESAME SEEDS**

1 ...... **SCALLION, CHOPPED FINE**

1 Score the fish 4 times diagonally on each side. Rub the sides with salt and let stand for 15 minutes.

2 Prepare the marinating sauce. Mix together the oil, soy sauce, chili powder, garlic, pepper, sesame seeds and scallion. Mix briskly and rub half of the sauce onto one side of the fish. Set aside for 15 minutes.

3 Broil over charcoal or in a gas or electric broiler for 5 minutes on each side of the fish. Remove, turn, and add the balance of the marinade to the other side of the fish. Return to the broiler for 2 more minutes.

Serve warm with rice and an assortment of side dishes.

Serves 4.

Seng Sun Bulgogi

The Bulgogi style of Korean barbecue is famous. Foreigners are most
familiar with the Korean cuisine by its barbecues — especially beef
and chicken. Here is the fillet of fish version.

> 1 ...... **TEASPOON SALT**
> 1 ¹/₂ ..... **POUNDS FILLET OF SEA BASS,
> RED SNAPPER, FLOUNDER OR
> SIMILAR FISH, CUT INTO 4 PIECES
> WITH THE SKIN**

> *Spice Paste*
> 1 ...... **TEASPOON SOY SAUCE**
> 2 ...... **TEASPOONS GOCHU JANG PASTE**
> 1 ...... **TEASPOON SUGAR**
> ¹/₄ ...... **TEASPOON BLACK PEPPER**
> 1 ...... **TEASPOON TOASTED SESAME SEEDS**
> 1 ...... **TEASPOON KOREAN SESAME OIL**
> 1 ...... **TEASPOON WHITE OR RICE WINE**
> 2 ...... **TABLESPOONS CHOPPED SCALLION**
> 1 ...... **GARLIC CLOVE, CHOPPED FINE**
> 1 ...... **TEASPOON MINCED FRESH GINGER**

1 Sprinkle salt over the fish fillet of choice and let stand uncovered in
the refrigerator overnight to dry out somewhat. Turn the pieces over
once during this time.

2 To prepare the spice paste, mix paste ingredients together. Rub the
paste into the fish pieces. Let stand for ¹/₂ hour, then broil over charcoal or in a gas or electric oven broiler for 5 minutes.

Serve warm with rice and side dishes of your choice.

Serves 4.

Seng Son Jim

The Seng Son Jim is first steamed, then spiced and finally lightly fried to incorporate all the flavors. Elaborately garnished, the whole fish with head and tail attached is served up with considerable flair. Semi-hot chili and ginger provide emphasis in the Korean manner.

1 1/2 .... **POUNDS WHOLE SALTWATER FISH SUCH AS CORVINA, RED SNAPPER OR SEA BASS**

1 ...... **TEASPOON SALT, OR TO TASTE**

1 ...... **TABLESPOON CHOPPED GINGER**

1/4 ..... **TEASPOON PEPPER**

1 ...... **TABLESPOON WHITE OR RICE WINE**

1 ...... **TABLESPOON CORNSTARCH**

2 ...... **DRIED MUSHROOMS, SOAKED IN WATER FOR 1 HOUR, DRAINED AND SHREDDED**

2 ...... **GARLIC CLOVES, CHOPPED**

2 ...... **OUNCES BEEFSTEAK, SHREDDED**

1 ...... **SCALLION, SLICED VERY THIN**

1 ...... **RED AND 1 GREEN SEMI-HOT CHILI, SEEDED AND SHREDDED**

2 ...... **TABLESPOONS GRATED CARROT**

1 ...... **TEASPOON KOREAN SESAME OIL**

1 ...... **TABLESPOON SOY SAUCE**

CORN OIL FOR PANFRYING

1 ...... **EGG, SEPARATED**

1 ...... **HARD-COOKED EGG, PEELED AND SLICED**

1 Pull out the gills from the fish. With fingers, chopsticks or fork pull out the stomach and any interior contents of the fish. Do not cut the fish open; perform surgery through the head. Rinse the fish thoroughly with cold water and drain. Cut about 4 diagonal slices up to the center bone (do not cut through) on both sides of the fish from head to tail.
2 Mix together the salt, ginger, pepper and wine to make the seasoning mixture. Pat this mix over the skin on both sides of the fish and set aside for 1/2 hour. Then sprinkle the cornstarch on both sides of the fish and steam in a Chinese-style steamer for 15 minutes.

3 Mix the mushrooms, garlic, steak, scallion, chilies, carrot, sesame oil and soy sauce together. Stir-fry these items in a wok or skillet over moderate heat for about 5 minutes. Push this garnish into the cuts on the fish.

4 Heat the corn oil in a skillet and panfry the steamed and garnished fish over moderate heat for 1 minute on each side. Remove the fish to a serving platter.

5 Beat the egg white and yolk separately and prepare a thin omelet of each in a skillet with the smallest amount of oil. Cool, then shred both omelets. Scatter each one over the fish in contrasting colors and place the sliced hard-cooked egg around the edge.

Serve warm with rice, kimchi and side dishes.

Serves 4 or 5.

Daegu Jiri

CODFISH HOT POT

Cod is generally cooked during the cool seasons from autumn through spring. It is the time of year when Korean thoughts turn to codfish in its culinary variety: soups, hot pots and kimchi. Here is a family-style preparation that can be increased for larger gatherings.

5	**CUPS WATER**
2	**POUNDS FRESH COD, CUT ACROSS INTO 1-INCH-WIDE SLICES WITH THE CENTER BONE IN**
1/2	**POUND KOREAN RADISH, CUT INTO 1-INCH SQUARES 1/2 INCH THICK**
1	**SMALL CARROT, CUT INTO 1-INCH-LONG DIAGONAL SLICES**
1/4	**POUND BEAN SPROUTS, HEADS AND TAILS REMOVED**
1/4	**POUND FRESH WILD MUSHROOMS, HALVED**
1	**SOFT SOYBEAN CAKE (TUBU), CUT INTO 6 EQUAL PIECES**
1/2	**MEDIUM-SIZE SWEET RED PEPPER, CUT INTO 6 PIECES**
1/2	**INCH OF FRESH GINGER, SLICED THIN**
2	**GARLIC CLOVES, SLICED THIN**
2	**TEASPOONS SALT, OR TO TASTE**
1/4	**POUND WATERCRESS STEMS AND LEAVES**
1	**SCALLION, CUT INTO 1-INCH PIECES**

1 Bring the water to a boil in a large pan over moderate heat. Add the cod, radish and carrot first, then the bean sprouts, mushrooms, tubu and sweet red pepper as the pot continues to boil. Add the ginger, garlic and salt and simmer for 15 minutes, which is enough to cook all the ingredients.

2 When ready to serve add the watercress and the scallion and serve immediately.

Serves 6 with rice.

NOTE: *Fish heads are popular and in demand in Korea for soups and stews. Should you be able to obtain the codfish head, then by all means include it in the hot pot, first removing the gills.*

Al Jigae

FISH ROE AND MUSHROOMS

Koreans prefer the roe of whiting, something not always easy to find even
during the spring season. I have discovered that the flounder roe,
which is easily available in large quantities, is inexpensive and has
a fine texture and flavor, and makes a good substitute.

3	CUPS WATER
1	TEASPOON SALT
1	TABLESPOON ANCHOVY POWDER
6	PIECES OF FLOUNDER ROE, ABOUT 1 1/2 POUNDS
1	OUNCE GROUND BEEF OR JULIENNE STEAK STRIPS
1	SMALL ONION, SLICED THIN (1/3 CUP)
7 OR 8	FRESH MUSHROOMS, WELL RINSED, SLICED
1/2	CUP JULIENNE STRIPS OF KOREAN RADISH
4	SCALLIONS, CUT INTO 3-INCH PIECES
1/4	TEASPOON PEPPER

Put the water, salt, anchovy powder, roe and beef in a pan and bring
to a boil over high heat. Add the onion, mushrooms, radish, scallions
and pepper. Bring to a boil, cover the pan, and cook over low heat for
15 minutes.

Serve warm.

Serves 4 with white rice.

Deahup Yang Nyom Gui

STUFFED CLAMS IN THE SHELL

People who live on a peninsula, like the Koreans, are dependent on the harvest that the sea presents, such as these large clams. The point here is to capture the essence of the clam meat and the natural liquid of a sealed clam. Opened with care, seasoned, chopped and combined with other ingredients, the clams are returned to the shell whence they came. They are then broiled, baked or roasted. Who could ask for anything more?

Clams

2 .... LARGE CLAMS, EACH 3 OR 4 INCHES ACROSS
1 ...... EGG, HARD-COOKED, SHELLED
1/2 ...... HARD CHINESE BEAN CURD, MASHED
2 ...... OUNCES BEEFSTEAK , SHREDDED

Seasoning

2 ...... TABLESPOONS SOY SAUCE
1/2 ...... TEASPOON HOT RED CHILI POWDER
1 ...... GARLIC CLOVE, CHOPPED
1/2 ...... TEASPOON CHOPPED FRESH GINGER
2 ...... TABLESPOONS SHREDDED SCALLIONS
1 ...... TEASPOON SUGAR
1 ...... TEASPOON KOREAN SESAME OIL
1 ...... TABLESPOON TOASTED SESAME SEEDS
1/8 ...... TEASPOON PEPPER

1 Scrub the clamshells well with a brush. Pour 1/4 cup hot water into a pan or skillet and bring it to a boil over moderate heat. Place the clams in the water, which continues to boil. When the shells have opened about 1/4 inch wide, remove the clams immediately and continue the opening with a dull knife or your fingers if possible. The inner liquid should be caught in a bowl, the clam pulled from the shell and the small dark stomach discarded. Chop the clam meat and combine with the liquid. Set aside. Reserve the 4 shells.
2 Chop the yolk and white of the egg separately and set aside.
3 Mix the seasoning ingredients together. Add the egg white and yolk, the mashed bean curd, steak, clam meat and liquid and combine everything together.
4 Stuff each shell with an equal amount of the stuffing. Broil under a gas or electric broiler or over charcoal until bubbling and brown, about 4 minutes, or they could be roasted in the oven at 350°F. for 20 minutes.

Serve warm with steamed rice.

Serves 4 as an appetizer.

Keh Sulchun

The moment you enter the Song Jook Hun Restaurant in Kwangju tranquility prevails. Removing your shoes, you step into a small courtyard filled with plants and trees, and up onto the raised platforms that make up the private dining areas. The elegantly polished wood floors, low tables and floor mats for seating add to the ambience of good taste and serenity. There is none of the bustle of an open public place, all is private and discreet.

This restaurant, whose name can be translated as meaning "loyal, sturdy and firm—not weak like the pine tree," is an old traditional restaurant of five rooms, filled with antique screens, calligraphy, genre paintings. It is not a restored or renovated house as one might suspect, but was built as a restaurant. The owner, Kim Bo Ok, is an attractive young woman of the region, whose mother and grandmother were the owners before her.

Originally the restaurant featured food and recipes of the Choson (Yi) dynasty (1392-1910), but recently the menu has been expanded to include more familiar regional dishes. The chef is a man—not common in Korea—but he has several assistants who are women.

I was served 50 different dishes, some of which are not usually served to the public—exquisite oyster roe and so-called krill liver (which is actually not a fish liver but a collection of miscellaneous tiny sea creatures including transparent miniature shrimps), but very little meat (only one small beef patty) and an emphasis on seafood, greens and vegetables, all with potent seasonings. Many of these offerings, small portions for two, were served in white porcelain bowls—a dramatic background for the ingredients.

Other dishes included a jellyfish salad in a sweet vinegar dressing; a firm and chewy roasted fish roe; sweet barley cake for a palate refresher; cold snails with a piquant dipping sauce; fried zucchini in batter; wild sesame leaves (perilla) with several fillings to make into sandwiches; and a delectable skate dish. There was an emphasis on variety of ingredients and also of flavors, but all dishes were served in modest quantities. A stir-fry of sweet potato leaves; ground shrimp reformed into its original shape and fried—the list is endless and it was all extraordinarily inventive but defies description to the uninitiated.

The owner and her assistant sat with us from time to time to explain the dishes as they appeared, many from the Yi dynasty. Since some of the foods were specialties of the region, they were not generally known even to Koreans.

(Continued next page)

The friendly and informative public relations of this low-keyed, serene restaurant, with its traditional values, are those of an exclusive eating house that does not provide "private" entertainment. It is one of the culinary jewels of Korea.

Here is their recipe for Crab Cake—one made from fresh crabs steamed right at the restaurant.

$\frac{1}{2}$......	**CUP COOKED RICE**
$\frac{1}{2}$......	**CUP FLAKED CRABMEAT**
2	**TABLESPOONS FINE-CHOPPED ONION**
1	**GARLIC CLOVE, CRUSHED**
2	**TABLESPOONS GRATED CARROT**
$\frac{1}{8}$......	**TEASPOON PEPPER**
	CORN OIL FOR PANFRYING

1 Mash the rice well and mix it with the crabmeat, onion, garlic, carrot and pepper. Prepare 4 patties about 3 inches in diameter and $\frac{3}{8}$ inch thick.

2 Heat the oil in a skillet and brown the patties over moderate heat for 2 or 3 minutes on each side. Drain briefly on paper towels.

Serve warm or at room temperature.

Makes 4 patties as a side dish.

Gye Tang

CRAB STEW

The people who live in the West and South of Korea have an almost unlimited supply of seafood: the western waters are not deep and produce millions of crabs, while the eastern seas are very deep and provide the larger fish. This crab stew is a favorite everywhere.

That Koreans do not eat soft-shell crabs, a seasonal delicacy in Maryland and the eastern shores of the United States, was an astonishing discovery to me, since everything else that emerges from the sea is consumed.

2	**LIVE CRABS**
1	**TABLESPOON CHOPPED GARLIC**
1	**TABLESPOON GOCHU JANG PASTE**
2	**TABLESPOONS SOY SAUCE**
1 TO 2 ...	**TEASPOONS RED CHILI POWDER, TO TASTE**
1	**TEASPOON SALT**
1/8	**TEASPOON BLACK PEPPER**
2	**CUPS WATER**
1	**MEDIUM-SIZE ONION, CHOPPED COARSE (1/2 CUP)**
3 OR 4 ...	**SEMI-HOT GREEN CHILIES, SEEDED, SLICED DIAGONALLY**
1	**POUND ZUCCHINI, CUT INTO 3/4-INCH TRIANGLES OR CUBES**
3	**SCALLIONS, CUT DIAGONALLY INTO 2-INCH PIECES**
	A FEW SPRIGS OF CHRYSANTHEMUM LEAVES

1 Put the crabs into the refrigerator for 2 hours so that they become less active and do not pinch so fiercely. Then scrub them well in cold water with a firm brush. Pull off the upper shell and leave it whole. Remove and discard the inner stomach of the crab. Cut the body and legs into 6 to 8 pieces.

2 Mix together the seasonings: garlic, gochu jang, soy sauce, red chili powder, salt and black pepper. Put the water into a pan; add the seasonings and onion. Bring to a boil and cook over low heat for 10 minutes.

(Continued next page)

3 Add the crab, green chilies, zucchini and scallions, cover the pan and cook over moderate heat for 10 minutes. Uncover, add the chrysanthemum, and remove the pan from the heat. Let stand for 10 minutes more, covered.

Serve the stew warm with the customary white rice. Whiskey, beer or the farm-style rice wine, mukhuli, is served with the stew.

Serves 4 to 6.

Gye Muchim

HIGHLY SEASONED RAW CRAB

A *muchim* is a "mixture" and it is a most appropriate name for this crab dish. It is not a preparation eaten as a main course but as a side dish that is tasted along with other foods. Marinating the crab in the vividly spiced soy sauce ensures a penetrating flavor. Also, and equally important is the fact that the salt in the soy sauce which covers the crab pieces, softens the shells and inner meat. The result is a marvelously melting texture when one chews the crab pieces; the meat dissolves in the mouth and the shells are crushed and discarded.

4 ...... **LIVE CRABS**
3 ...... **TABLESPOONS SUGAR**
2 ...... **TABLESPOONS SESAME SEEDS**
2 ...... **TABLESPOONS KOREAN SESAME OIL**
4 ...... **TABLESPOONS CHOPPED SCALLIONS, GREEN PART ONLY**
3 ...... **TABLESPOONS CHOPPED GARLIC**
1 ...... **TABLESPOON CHOPPED GINGER**
2 ...... **TABLESPOONS HOT RED CHILI POWDER**
1 ...... **MEDIUM-SIZE ONION, CUT INTO THIN SLICES (1 CUP)**
3 ...... **RED AND 3 GREEN SEMI-HOT CHILIES, SEEDED, SLICED THIN DIAGONALLY**
1 ...... **CUP SOY SAUCE**

1 Scrub the crabs with a firm brush to clean. Remove and discard the upper shell. Only the body and legs of the crab are used. Do not dislodge the orange crab roe that clings to the inner shell and contents. Cut the body into halves, then each half into 2 or 3 pieces including the legs.

2 Mix together the sugar, sesame seeds and oil, scallions, garlic, ginger, red chili powder, onion and chilies. Mix this with the soy sauce, then strain the seasoned sauce into a marinating bowl. Reserve the seasoning ingredients. Mix the crab pieces in the sauce and marinate, covered, in the refrigerator for 24 hours.

3 The next day add the seasoning ingredients to the crab and soy sauce, mix well, and serve at room temperature with steamed rice and an assortment of other Korean dishes.

Serves 4 to 6 as a side dish.

Gye Jim

STEAMED CRAB STUFFED IN THE SHELL

Crabmeat clings to the many interstices of the shell and it is difficult to extract the uncooked meat. The result is worth the effort, however, for this festive and elegant dish. Color is a predominant consideration in the garnishes: the red crab shell, green of the chrysanthemum leaves, white and yellow omelet shreds, the feathery red chili strands and the green cucumber skin. The Gye Jim is an aesthetic and culinary gem.

4	**FRESH CRABS (PREFERABLY BLUE CRAB)**
1	**TEASPOON SOY SAUCE**
1	**TABLESPOON TOASTED SESAME SEEDS**
1	**TABLESPOON CHOPPED SCALLION, GREEN PART ONLY**
1	**GARLIC CLOVE, CHOPPED**
½	**TEASPOON SALT**
1	**TEASPOON KOREAN SESAME OIL**
1	**HARD BEAN CURD, WELL DRIED ON PAPER TOWELS AND MASHED**
2	**EGGS**
3	**OUNCES BEAN SPROUTS, BOILED IN WATER FOR 5 SECONDS, DRAINED, LIQUID SQUEEZED OUT, CHOPPED**
¼	**POUND BEEFSTEAK, CHOPPED BY HAND (NOT GROUND)**
1	**TABLESPOON FLOUR**

Garnishes

1	**KIRBY CUCUMBER, SHREDDED, SALTED FOR 10 MINUTES WITH ½ TEASPOON SALT, SQUEEZED DRY**
2	**MANNA LICHEN DRIED MUSHROOMS (*GYROPHORA ESCULENTA*), SOAKED IN HOT WATER UNTIL SOFT, DRAINED, SHREDDED (OPTIONAL)**
2	**SPRIGS OF CHRYSANTHEMUM LEAVES**
10	**HOT RED CHILI THREADS**

1 Pull off the upper shell of the crab and reserve it for stuffing. Rinse out the bottom shell; discard the stomach. Remove the crab eggs if any and meticulously pull out the crab meat as best as you can. Empty the bottom shell of any small meat particles. Set aside the meat.

2 Mix together the soy sauce, sesame seeds, scallion, garlic, salt and sesame oil. Mix this with the crab meat, bean curd, 1 beaten egg, bean sprouts and beefsteak into a smooth mixture. Set aside.

3 Separate the white and yolk of the other egg and prepare 2 omelets, white and yellow. Cool and slice into thin strips.

4 Dust the interior of the top shells with the flour and shake out the excess. Stuff the crab shells to the top with the crabmeat mixture. Put the shells in a Chinese-style steamer with the crab claws and steam over moderate heat for 15 minutes. Remove and cool for 5 minutes.

5 Put the chrysanthemum leaves on the bottom of a serving platter. Place the steamed crabs on top and garnish with strips of color, the yellow and white omelet strips, the julienned cucumber, the mushrooms if used and the chili threads.

Serve cold or at room temperature.

Serves 4.

Saeoo Jchim

STEAMED SHRIMPS WITH GARNISHES

Koreans like to garnish their dishes with very thin strips, literally threads, of carrots, cucumber peel, tree ears, semi-hot chili both green and red, yellow and white omelets or anything else that lends itself to this treatment. Contrast is what they want and these strips of color, meticulously placed, satisfy this need. In keeping with the Korean philosophy of greaseless foods, the shrimps thus decorated are steamed (not fried) for several minutes, just enough to turn them pink and add another color.

CORN OIL FOR FRYING OMELETS

1 .... **EGG, SEPARATED**

5 .... **SHRIMPS WITH THE HEAD, ABOUT 1/2 POUND**

4 OR 5 .... **DRIED TREE EARS, SOAKED IN WATER FOR 1 HOUR, DRAINED, SLICED VERY THIN**

1 .... **SMALL KIRBY CUCUMBER, RINSED IN SALT WATER TO INTENSIFY THE GREEN COLOR, THE SKIN CUT OFF 1/8 INCH THICK AND SLICED VERY THIN (USE THE PULP FOR ANOTHER PURPOSE)**

2-INCH.... **PIECE OF CARROT, SLICED VERY THIN, CUT INTO 1-INCH-LONG STRIPS**

1 Put a nonstick skillet over low heat and oil lightly. Pour in the egg white, lightly beaten with a few grains of salt. Swirl the skillet so that the egg white covers the pan in a thin layer. Fry for 1 minute, just enough to make the omelet firm, then lift the edges and turn it over, frying for another few seconds. Turn out on a cutting board and cool completely. Do the same for the egg yolk. Then cut each omelet into very thin slices 1 inch long. Set aside.

2 Remove the head of each shrimp and set aside. Peel off the shrimp shell up to the last segment. Devein each shrimp and slice it open butterfly style but do not cut through. Now cut the shrimp very lightly all around the edges. This is supposed to give a larger surface area and the illusion when steamed of a larger shrimp than it really is. The tail and last segment of the shell are intact and the flesh is spread out into an oval.

3 Decorate the shrimp, starting at the tail end. In this order, first place several slices of the tree ears horizontally across the shrimp. Then add 3 slices of the white omelet, followed by 3 slices of the yellow omelet. Now place 3 slices of the cucumber peel, 3 slices of carrot, alternating the colors.

4 Place the shrimps on a round, heatproof platter, tails outward. Now place the reserved shrimp heads upright, standing on end and clustered together in the center of the platter. When the water has started to boil in a Chinese-style steamer, put the shrimp platter on the steam tray which is perforated to allow the steam to circulate. Steam for 3 minutes and remove.

Serve warm or at room temperature as a cocktail appetizer or as one of the dishes in a Korean meal. There is no sauce or dip. The heads are to be chewed but not swallowed to extract the sweet broth.

Serves 2 or more as a side dish.

Saeoo Gui

To prepare shrimps this way is an extravagance because, although expensive in Korea, it is the very large shrimps that are preferred. They would probably weigh about 3 ounces each—an impressive size—and would be purchased with the heads on, if possible. Of course small shrimps may be selected but would not have the impact that giants have.

> 5 ...... **LARGE SHRIMPS TO WEIGH AT LEAST
> 1 POUND ALTOGETHER**
> ¼ ...... **POUND GROUND BEEF**
> ½ ...... **FIRM CHINESE-STYLE BEAN CURD, MASHED**
> ½ ...... **TEASPOON SALT**
> ⅛ ...... **TEASPOON PEPPER**
> ¼ ...... **TEASPOON SUGAR**
> 1 ...... **TEASPOON FLOUR**
> 1 ...... **TEASPOON SOY SAUCE**
> ½ ...... **TEASPOON KOREAN SESAME OIL**

1 Shell and devein the shrimps in the same method as found in Saeoo Jchim (see previous recipe). Reserve the heads.

2 Mix well together the beef, bean curd, salt, pepper and sugar. Sprinkle about ¼ teaspoon flour over each butterflied shrimp. Take 1 tablespoon or a bit more of the beef mixture and shape a thin oval cake to cover the center portion of a shrimp. Sprinkle the soy sauce and sesame oil over the filling.

3 Place the stuffed shrimps and heads on a lightly oiled metal grill in a gas or electric broiler and broil for about 5 minutes, which is enough to cook the beef and shrimps.

Place the shrimps on a platter, tails outward like the spokes of a wheel. The grilled heads are to be standing upright in the center of the platter.

Serve warm as an appetizer or with other foods in a lunch or dinner.

Serves 5 as a side dish.

Hae San Mool Jungol

The title can only hint at this very grand celebratory dish that is an
encyclopedia of Korean culinary ideas and style. The 21 ingredients
in the assortment are arranged in groups in an aesthetic manner
according to their contrasting colors. For example, the zucchini slices
are placed next to the noodles, which are next to the oysters, which
are next to the carrots, and so on. The emphasis is on quality, quantity
and variety. (It is not unconventional for Koreans to cook beef and
seafood together.) The intensity of the broth, which has been seasoned
with the 10 different paste ingredients, blends it all into one.

Seasoning Paste

- 2 .... TABLESPOONS GOCHU JANG
- 1 TO 2 .... TABLESPOONS HOT RED CHILI POWDER, TO TASTE
- 2 .... TABLESPOONS SOY SAUCE
- 1 .... TABLESPOON CHOPPED GARLIC
- 1 .... TABLESPOON CHOPPED SCALLION
- 1 .... TABLESPOON TOASTED SESAME SEEDS
- 1 .... TEASPOON KOREAN SESAME OIL
- 1/2 ...... TEASPOON CHOPPED FRESH GINGER
- 1 .... TEASPOON SALT, OR TO TASTE
- 1/4 ...... TEASPOON BLACK PEPPER

Assorted Ingredients

- 1/2 ...... POUND THIN (FOR TENDERNESS) OCTOPUS TENTACLES, CUT INTO 2-INCH PIECES
- 1/2 ...... POUND BEEFSTEAK, CUT INTO JULIENNE STRIPS
- 4 .... SMALL CLAMS IN THE SHELL, WELL SCRUBBED
- 4 .... LARGE SHRIMPS, PEELED AND DEVEINED
- 1 .... CRAB, CUT INTO 4 PIECES
- 1 .... SMALL SQUID, CLEANED, CUT INTO 2-INCH PIECES, BLANCHED IN BOILING WATER FOR 5 SECONDS
- 1/2 ...... POUND FRESH SHUCKED OYSTERS, RINSED IN SALTED WATER, DRAINED

(Continued next page)

½ ...... **POUND ANY SALTWATER
FISH FILLET, CUT INTO 2-INCH
PIECES, OR THE WHOLE FISH
WITH HEAD, IN ½-INCH SLICES**

½ ...... **POUND ZUCCHINI, CUT INTO
HALF-MOON SLICES ¼ INCH THICK**

1 .... **SMALL CARROT, CUT INTO
2-INCH-LONG JULIENNE STRIPS**

6 .... **SCALLIONS, CUT INTO 2-INCH PIECES**

¼ ...... **POUND FRESH MUSHROOMS, HALVED**

1 .... **LARGE ONION (½ POUND), SLICED THICK**

¼ ...... **POUND RICE CAKE, CUT INTO
⅛-INCH-THICK SLICES**

1 .... **CAN (8 OUNCES) BAMBOO SHOOTS,
CUT INTO ¼-INCH-THICK SLICES**

6 .... **SLICES OF PREPARED FISH CAKE,
CUT INTO ¼-INCH-THICK SLICES**

¼ ...... **POUND KOREAN RADISH, CUT INTO
¼-INCH-THICK SLICES**

2 .... **GREEN AND 2 RED FRESH SEMI-HOT
CHILIES, SEEDED, CUT INTO
DIAGONAL ¼-INCH-THICK SLICES**

¼ ...... **POUND FRESH EGG NOODLES,
BLANCHED IN BOILING WATER FOR
½ MINUTE, DRAINED**

2 .... **CUPS BEEF BROTH OR WATER
A FEW SPRIGS OF WELL-RINSED
CHRYSANTHEMUM LEAVES**

1 Mix seasoning paste ingredients together and set aside.

2 In a deep 12-inch skillet with a cover, align the assortment of all ingredients except broth and chrysanthemum leaves in this order: The hard vegetables such as radish, carrot and bamboo shoots line the bottom of the pan. Then place individual groups of the other ingredients around the perimeter of the pan and in the center. Nothing is scattered about but all are placed in a specific spot.

3 Place the seasoning on the top of the ingredients in the center of the pan. Bring the mixture to a simmer over moderate heat for 3 minutes. Then add the 2 cups beef broth or water around the edge of the pan. Bring this to a boil, then reduce the heat to low, cover the pan, and cook for ½ hour. The seasoning paste will filter down and throughout the pan during the cooking process. At the end of the time, add the sprigs of chrysanthemum leaves and cook for 1 minute more.

(Continued next page)

4 Each person will help himself from the steaming pan, selecting a sampling of the ingredients and a spoonful of the thick, rich broth. Several helpings are usually taken.

Serves 8 persons or more with white rice.

NOTE: *Rice cakes are long rolls of cooked, pressed rice that are smooth on the outside and moist on the inside. They are very similar to the* lontong *of Indonesia. The rice cakes can be purchased in Korean groceries.*

Nagchi Foee

The original recipe and custom call for the octopus slices to be raw but I find them difficult to chew and rather rubbery. The cooked, tender slices are more acceptable to western taste.

½...... **POUND COOKED OCTOPUS, CUT INTO 1 ½-INCH-LONG, ½-INCH-WIDE SLICES**

½...... **THE QUANTITY OF NAGCHI BOEKUM SAUCE (SEE FOLLOWING RECIPE) MIXED WITH 1 TABLESPOON CIDER VINEGAR**

Arrange the octopus slices on a serving platter. Put the dipping sauce in a bowl and serve with the octopus. Dip and eat.

Serve cold or at room temperature as a side dish or unconventional appetizer.

Serves 4.

Nagchi Boekum

OCTOPUS IN A HOT SAUCE

Anything that swims in the seas around Korea can be—and is—eaten. A fine example is this Nagchi Boekum. The lowly octopus with its softly textured flesh still full of the flavor of the sea is stir-fried in a robust sauce.

The giant scallion used here grows as large as a leek in Korea; I have seen them as long as 30 inches. They are sometimes available in the United States but small ones make an acceptable substitute.

Sauce

1	**TABLESPOON CHOPPED FRESH GINGER**
1	**TABLESPOON CHOPPED GARLIC**
2	**TABLESPOONS GOCHU JANG**
1/8	**TEASPOON BLACK PEPPER**
1 TO 2 ...	**TEASPOONS HOT RED CHILI POWDER**
2	**TEASPOONS KOREAN SESAME OIL**
2	**TEASPOONS TOASTED SESAME SEED SALT**
2	**TABLESPOONS SUGAR**

Octopus

1	**POUND OCTOPUS (A SMALL ONE)**
4	**TABLESPOONS SALT**
2	**TABLESPOONS CORN OIL**
1	**GIANT SCALLION OR 5 STANDARD SCALLIONS, CUT DIAGONALLY INTO 1-INCH SLICES**

1 Mix the sauce ingredients together and set aside.
2 Rinse the octopus thoroughly in cold water. Put it into a bowl with the salt and 2 cups water. Mix and let stand for 10 minutes. This will remove any excessive fish aroma. Then swirl the octopus around in the salty liquid for a minute, drain thoroughly and rinse in cold water to remove any sand. Pull out the stomach contents, cut out the ink sack and eyes, and trim 2 inches off of the tentacle tips. Rinse again in cold water.

Or, purchase the octopus ready-to-cook from your neighborhood Korean fish market. Rinse in cold water before using.
3 Pour enough water to cover the octopus into a large pan. Bring

(Continued next page)

to a boil and add the octopus either whole or in pieces, and cook over moderate heat for $^1/_2$ hour or a bit more until very tender. Drain. Cut into thin 1$^1/_2$-inch-long pieces, and set aside.

4 Heat the oil in a wok or large skillet, add the sauce and stir-fry over moderate heat for 1 minute. Add the scallions, stir-fry a few seconds, then add $^1/_4$ cup water and cook for 2 minutes. Add the octopus slices and continue to stir-fry for 2 minutes. Do not overcook.

Serve warm with white rice and side dishes of your choice.

Serves 6.

Ojingau *Feu*

FRESH SQUID WITH DIP

Squid is one of the most popular seafoods in Korea—plentiful and cheap.
One can make this appetizer with fresh, raw squid lightly blanched
in boiling water or tender-cooked squid, but not overdone or it will
be tough. Many Koreans prefer the raw squid since it retains the
aroma and taste of the sea.

2 ...... **LARGE SQUID, ABOUT 1 ½ POUNDS**

1 TO 2.... **TABLESPOONS HOT RED CHILI
POWDER, TO TASTE**

1 ...... **TABLESPOON CHOPPED GARLIC**

1 ...... **TABLESPOON CHOPPED SCALLION,
GREEN PART ONLY**

1 ...... **TEASPOON FINE-CHOPPED
FRESH GINGER**

1 ...... **TABLESPOON CRUSHED TOASTED
SESAME SEEDS**

1 ...... **TABLESPOON WHITE OR CIDER VINEGAR**

1 ...... **TABLESPOON SUGAR**

1 ...... **TABLESPOON KOREAN SESAME OIL**

1 ...... **FRESH SEMI-HOT GREEN CHILI,
SEEDED AND CHOPPED FINE**

1 ...... **FRESH SEMI-HOT RED CHILI, SEEDED
AND CHOPPED FINE**

1 Clean the squid in the conventional manner; use the tubular body
only. Reserve the tentacles and trimmings for another use. Cut the
squid body into strips ½ inch wide and 3 inches long.
2 Thoroughly mix together the chili powder, garlic, scallion, ginger,
sesame seeds, vinegar, sugar and sesame oil to make a dip.

To serve, put the squid in one dish, the dip in another and the fresh
chilies in another. Diners will help themselves to the dip according to
taste, and will sprinkle as much chili as is tolerable over that.

Serve cool or at room temperature.

Serves 4.

Ojingau *Po Muchim*

Off the coast of eastern Korea lies Ullungdo Island, jutting out of the beautiful turquoise water of the South China Sea. There one can see large squid strung on bamboo poles, drying in the sun, their color changing from chalk white to burnished brown. Dried squid is often sold at Korean newsstands where one sees commuters munching on pieces pulled off the flattened brown body, tentacles and all. Delicious!

1 ...... **POUND DRIED SQUID, SHREDDED (SEE NOTE)**
1 ...... **TABLESPOON HOT RED CHILI POWDER**
1 OR 2 ... **TABLESPOONS SOY SAUCE, TO TASTE**
1 ...... **TABLESPOON SUGAR**
3 ...... **GARLIC CLOVES, CHOPPED FINE**
1 ...... **TABLESPOON TOASTED SESAME SEEDS**
1 ...... **TEASPOON KOREAN SESAME OIL**

1 Soak the dried squid in cold water for 10 minutes. Drain well and set aside.
2 Mix together the hot chili powder, soy sauce, sugar, garlic, sesame seeds and oil. Toss well with the squid shreds.

Serve cool or at room temperature as a side dish.

Serves 6 to 8.

NOTE: *Dried squid is sold in Korean groceries packed in plastic bags. Once the bag has been opened, the squid should be refrigerated.*

Ojingau Soonday

This is not a sausage as we think of it, but sausage is the literal translation.
The body of the squid provides the casing for the seasoned squid meat
and it is then steamed.

Seasoning Paste

1 .... **TABLESPOON CHOPPED GARLIC**

2 .... **TABLESPOONS CHOPPED SCALLION,
GREEN PART ONLY**

2 .... **FRESH SEMI-HOT RED CHILIES,
SEEDED, CHOPPED**

2 .... **FRESH SEMI-HOT GREEN CHILIES,
SEEDED, CHOPPED**

1 .... **TABLESPOON TOASTED SESAME SEEDS**

1 .... **TABLESPOON KOREAN SESAME OIL**

¼ .... **TEASPOON BLACK PEPPER**

1 TO 2 ..... **TEASPOONS SALT, TO TASTE**

Squid and Stuffing

2½ TO 3 ... **POUNDS SQUID, WITH BODIES
8 TO 10 INCHES LONG**

5 .... **TABLESPOONS FLOUR**

1 .... **HARD CHINESE-STYLE BEAN
CURD, MASHED**

½ .... **POUND MUNG BEAN SPROUTS,
PARBOILED IN WATER FOR 1 MINUTE,
SQUEEZED DRY AND CHOPPED**

1 .... **EGG, BEATEN**

1 First, mix the seasoning ingredients together and set aside.

2 Clean the squid, remove the stomach contents, pull off the thin black
skin, discard the eye in the tentacles. Rinse everything well in cold
water and drain. Chop the tentacles. Put about 1 tablespoon flour into
each squid body, shake well then turn out the excess. Set aside.

3 Mix together the bean curd, bean sprouts, remaining 1 tablespoon
flour, the egg and chopped tentacles. Stir in the seasoning paste. Fill
the squid body with the stuffing (but not too firm or full since it will
ooze out). Steaming will shrink the squid body so that the stuffing
should be sufficient to fill the body but not so much that it is forced out
during the steaming process. Close the end of the body with a wooden
skewer or firm toothpick.

(Continued next page)

4 Steam in a Chinese-style steamer over moderate heat for $^1/_2$ hour. Remove immediately and let the "sausage" cool so that it will become easier to slice. Then cut into $^1/_2$-inch-wide slices.

Serve warm or at room temperature with vinegar dip (2 tablespoons soy sauce mixed with 1 tablespoon cider or white vinegar), salads, kimchi and steamed rice.

Serves 4 to 6.

Ojingau Bokum

Another reason for the popularity of squid, besides its availability and low cost, is its suitability for combining with so many other ingredients and seasonings—with results pleasing to many dissimilar tastes. This stir-fry is a good example of a dish for those who like it mild, in great contrast to Chili-Hot Squid and Vegetable Stir-Fry on pages 199-200.

- 1/2 ...... POUND FRESH SQUID
- 3 ...... LARGE DRIED MUSHROOMS
- 2 ...... TEASPOONS CHOPPED FRESH GINGER
- 1 ...... TEASPOON WHITE OR RICE WINE
- 1 ...... TEASPOON CORNSTARCH
- 3 ...... CUPS WATER
- 2 ...... TABLESPOONS CORN OIL FOR STIR-FRYING
- 1 ...... GARLIC CLOVE, CHOPPED FINE
- 1 ...... SCALLION, CUT INTO 2-INCH PIECES, WHITE PART HALVED LENGTHWISE
- 1 ...... MEDIUM-SIZE CARROT, CUT INTO 2-INCH JULIENNE STRIPS
- 10 ..... SNOW PEAS, TRIMMED, SOAKED IN COLD .... WATER FOR 1/2 HOUR BEFORE USING
- 1/2 ...... TEASPOON SUGAR
- 1/2 ...... TEASPOON SALT, TO TASTE
- 2 ...... TEASPOONS SOY SAUCE
- 1/2 ...... TEASPOON KOREAN SESAME OIL

1 Clean the squid in conventional manner, removing the tentacles and pulling off the very thin black skin. Rinse very well in cold water. Cut the body tube into 2-inch-wide pieces. Cut each piece open and then cut into pieces 2 inches long and 1/2 inch wide. Score each piece lightly, diagonally from left to right sides. Reserve the tentacles for other dishes.

2 Soak the mushrooms in water to cover for 2 hours. Drain, cut into 3 equal parts. Discard the hard stems.

3 Mix the squid pieces with the ginger, wine and cornstarch and marinate for 15 minutes. Heat the water to a rapid boil and add the squid. When the water boils again, drain quickly and set squid aside. The squid pieces will curl up in a decorative manner and remain white.

(Continued next page)

4 Heat the oil in a wok or large skillet. Add the garlic and scallion and stir-fry for 1 minute. Add the mushrooms, carrot and snow peas and stir-fry for 1 minute. Then add the sugar, salt, soy sauce, sesame oil and squid and continue to stir-fry for 3 minutes.

At this point, add more salt if needed. Do not overcook or the squid will toughen and the vegetables will lose their bright colors.

Serve warm with rice, any number of salads and soup.

Serves 4.

Maewoon Ojingau Bokum

CHILI-HOT SQUID AND VEGETABLE STIR-FRY
WITH NOODLES

Chili powder supplemented by the ubiquitous gochu jang paste provides both heat and color to this popular stir-fry. Additional chili may be added to taste and tolerance, remembering that plain, white, sticky rice dilutes the intensity. Note that the squid and carrot are cut to approximately the same size for aesthetic reasons.

1	POUND FRESH SQUID (2 OR 3)
2	TABLESPOONS CORN OIL FOR STIR-FRYING, OR MORE
1/2	INCH OF FRESH GINGER, CHOPPED FINE
2	GARLIC CLOVES, CHOPPED FINE
1	LARGE CARROT, CUT INTO SLICES 2 INCHES LONG, 1/2 INCH WIDE AND 1/8 INCH THICK
1	MEDIUM-SIZE ONION, CUT INTO HALF-MOON SLICES
2	SCALLIONS, SLICED 2 INCHES LONG, THE THICK WHITE PART HALVED LENGTHWISE, THEN SLICED
1/2	TEASPOON SALT, OR TO TASTE
2	TEASPOONS SUGAR
1	TABLESPOON GOCHU JANG
1 TO 2	TEASPOONS HOT RED CHILI POWDER
1	TEASPOON TOASTED SESAME SEEDS
1/2	TEASPOON KOREAN SESAME OIL
2	TEASPOONS CORNSTARCH DILUTED IN 2 TABLESPOONS COLD WATER
3	OUNCES THIN WHITE JAPANESE WHEAT NOODLES

1 Clean the squid and cut them, including tentacles, into slices 2 inches long and 1/2 inch wide. Cut the squid's tubular body lengthwise into halves, open it up and then cut pieces to the desired size. **2** Heat the oil in a wok or large skillet, add the ginger and garlic and stir-fry over moderate heat for 1 minute. Add the squid, carrot and onion and continue to stir-fry for 1 minute, adding the scallions, salt and sugar as you fry and the natural liquid of the ingredients accumulates.

(Continued next page)

3 Make a well in the middle of the mixture and put in the gochu jang paste, chili powder, sesame seeds and oil, and the diluted cornstarch and mix everything together for 2 minutes.

4 In the meantime, bring 3 cups water to a rapid boil in a pan, add the noodles and cook for not more than 1 minute. Rinse under cold water.

To serve, put the squid mixture into a large round platter or bowl, make a well in the center and add the noodles. Serve at the table this way, then toss everything together in front of the guests or family. The diners can see the color and composition of the dish before it is mixed together, a Korean style of service in home or restaurant. Of course, if preferred it all may be mixed together in the kitchen and then served.

Serve warm with rice, salads and condiments in the Korean manner.

Serves 4 to 6.

Ojingau Bulgogi

Millions of squid are caught from the waters around the Korean peninsula. Bays, inlets and island waters provide rich fishing grounds for this, the most popular and the cheapest of seafoods. The phantasmagoric island of Ullungdo has proof, through historical records and an ancient grave on the island, of its early development; its fame, however, comes from the squid that enrich the fishermen and provide the folk on the Korean mainland an important part of their diet.

2½ TO 3	**POUNDS FRESH SQUID, WITH BODY SIZE OF 8 TO 9 INCHES**
2 TO 3	**TABLESPOONS GOCHU JANG PASTE, TO TASTE**
1	**TABLESPOON SOY SAUCE**
3	**TABLESPOONS CHOPPED SCALLION**
1	**TABLESPOON CHOPPED GARLIC**
1	**TABLESPOON SUGAR**
1½	**TABLESPOONS TOASTED SESAME SEEDS**
1	**TABLESPOON KOREAN SESAME OIL**
¼	**TEASPOON BLACK PEPPER**

1 Clean the squid, remove the very thin black skin, inner stomach and contents. Remove the tentacles and reserve for another use. Rinse the body well in cold water and drain.
2 Cut the body into 4 to 6 rectangles. Score each piece 3 times lengthwise and crosswise. Blanch each piece in boiling water for 3 seconds, then quickly remove and drain.
3 Prepare the seasoning. Mix into a paste all the ingredients except the squid, remembering that the gochu jang is a hot paste and should be added to taste. Mix the squid with the seasoning and let stand for ½ hour.
4 Broil the squid over charcoal or in a gas or electric broiler for only 2 minutes since squid toughens with excessive cooking. The squid may also be panfried with 1 teaspoon corn oil in a skillet over high heat, just enough to sear both sides of the rectangle. The barbecue, however, is the traditional method.

Serve warm with steamed rice.

Serves 4 to 6 persons with other dishes.

Meat and Poultry

In the past, those who had money were able to purchase as much meat and poultry as they wanted without economical restrictions. But in a country that relied on fish and all other kinds of edible seafood, meat was relegated to a food of luxury and special occasions. Formerly, all this was true, but now that Koreans have reached a degree of affluence never before achieved in their ancient or contemporary history, beef, chicken and pork are more frequently served at home and in restaurants and there are plenty of recipes now available.

Beef is the most prestigious and expensive meat. In earlier times domestic cattle were raised on farms in limited numbers. They were used primarily as bullocks in grinding seeds for oil on primitive stone wheels, as well as for tilling the soil. The use of cattle as food was only an adjunct to their use as beasts of burden. Now, with modern techniques, commercial dairies have been established and beef is available—but at a price. *Bulgogi,* the most popular beef dish, has reached the heights as a Korean culinary icon. Foreigners threading their way through a not always understandable Korean menu can count on *bulgogi* to meet their expectations.

Koreans living in the north close to the Chinese border are primarily pork eaters like the Chinese. Mountainous terrain, limited grazing space and frigid winters are features inhospitable to raising cattle. Pork is easier and therefore available and popular.

People in the south of Korea do not usually eat pork or chicken but prefer beef. Rules are sometimes meant to be broken as is proven by the excellent Samgyetang (Baby Chicken and Ginseng) which I enjoyed on Cheju Island in the extreme South of Korea.

The American kitchen will find that Korean meat and poultry dishes are easily prepared and accessible from a culinary point of view, reflecting the Korean tradition.

Pa-Kang Hoi

STEAK BUNDLE WITH SAUCE

Certain foods often become a ritual of the season in any culture. In Korea, the Steak Bundle is a ritual of the spring and has romantic overtones. The sauce, which is so important to this dish, is hot, sour and sweet (*cho-jang*) and has a classic combination of flavors. The steak itself, which is uncooked, is reminiscent of the steak tartare of Western cooking, except that the beef is not ground.

Sauce
- ½ ..... **CUP SOY SAUCE**
- 1 ...... **TABLESPOON GOCHU JANG**
- 1 ½..... **TABLESPOONS CIDER VINEGAR**
- 1 ½..... **TABLESPOONS SUGAR**
- 1 ...... **TEASPOON KOREAN SESAME OIL**
- 1 ...... **TEASPOON TOASTED SESAME SEEDS**
- 1 ...... **TEASPOON FINE-CHOPPED FRESH GINGER**
- 2 ...... **SCALLIONS, CHOPPED FINE**

Steak
- 2 ...... **KOREAN SCALLIONS**
- ½ ..... **TEASPOON SALT**
- 3 ...... **CUPS WATER**
- ½ ..... **POUND BEEF SIRLOIN OR FILLET STEAK**

1 Mix sauce ingredients together briskly to dissolve the sugar. Set aside.
2 Trim the root end of the scallions. Rinse well. Bring the salt and 3 cups water to a boil, add the scallions and cook over moderate heat for 3 or 4 minutes, or until soft and flexible. Drain and cool. Now pull off 1 scallion leaf at a time. If the green part is very wide, it may be split lengthwise. These will be the wrappers.
3 Cut the steak into strips about 3 inches long and ¼ inch wide. Place 1 scallion leaf flat on a cutting board. Put 1 steak strip on the white part of the leaf and fold the green part over front and back, to cover completely, and tie around the center of the strip like a belt around one's waist.
4 Divide the sauce into small individual Asian sauce dishes, one for each person. Place all the steak on a flat plate. Each guest selects a piece and dips it into the sauce generously.

Serve as a side dish or as an appetizer with drinks, if you wish.

Serves 4.

NOTE: *Adding a small amount of salt to green vegetables increases the intensity of the color. The scallion leaves on the bundle will appear more aesthetically pleasing.*

Bulgogi

This is one of Korea's most popular dishes. Beef is expensive so the barbecue (*bulgogi*) is not an everyday occurrence but is one of the most representative Korean foods and is often served to tourists.

In the old days, the thin slices of steak were marinated, then grilled over wood. When the flames died down and the coals were glowing red, the strips of beef were thrown on a rack over the coals for a minute or two, turned over and served while hot. Today, restaurants serve the *bulgogi* on table gas grills and the great flavor of country wood and smoke is missing. Nevertheless, the marinade has penetrated the beef and substantial flavor is retained. The modern home recipe also uses a somewhat different procedure.

1½..... **POUNDS BONELESS RIB STEAK, CUT INTO VERY THIN SLICES 5 TO 6 INCHES LONG BY 2 INCHES WIDE**

4 ...... **TEASPOONS SUGAR**

¼ ..... **CUP SOY SAUCE**

3 ...... **GARLIC CLOVES, CRUSHED OR CHOPPED FINE**

3 ...... **SCALLIONS, CUT INTO 1-INCH PIECES**

¼ ..... **TEASPOON PEPPER**

1 ...... **TEASPOON KOREAN SESAME OIL**

1 Mix the beef and sugar together. Let it rest for 2 minutes, then add the soy sauce, garlic, scallions, pepper and sesame oil. Toss the mixture well to integrate all the flavors, and let it stand at room temperature for a minimum of 1 hour (or overnight in the refrigerator) to allow the meat to mature.

2 Preheat a large, heavy skillet over moderate heat for 2 minutes. Add the beef slices, a few at a time, and sear them without oil for 2 or 3 minutes at most. Of course, in summer this may be done outdoors over charcoal.

An alternate method is to grill the beef in a very hot gas or electric broiler.

Serve immediately with white sticky rice and an assortment of side dishes.

Serves 6.

Kalbi Gui

Tender, piquant, thin-sliced rib steaks including the very tip end of bone, to be marinated in Korean style and then grilled, are easily the most popular and expensive cut of beef. But worth every cent!

8 .... **SLICES OF RIB STEAK (1 ½ POUNDS), CUT ABOUT 6 INCHES LONG, 3 INCHES WIDE AND ¼ INCH THICK, RINSED IN WATER, DRIED**

Marinade

2 .... **TEASPOONS WHITE OR RICE WINE**

2 .... **TEASPOONS SUGAR**

1 .... **TABLESPOON SOY SAUCE**

2 .... **LARGE GARLIC CLOVES, CRUSHED TO A PASTE OR CHOPPED FINE**

2 .... **SCALLIONS, CHOPPED FINE IN THE OLD METHOD OR SLICED INTO 2-INCH PIECES**

¼ ...... **TEASPOON PEPPER**

½ ...... **TEASPOON KOREAN SESAME OIL**

Wrappers

8 .... **LARGE LETTUCE LEAVES, ROMAINE, BOSTON OR OTHER LOOSE-LEAF VARIETY**

FRESH CHRYSANTHEMUM (SOOKGAT) LEAVES, IF AVAILABLE

2 .... **TABLESPOONS DENJAN AND 1 TABLESPOON GOCHU JANG MIXED TOGETHER (SAMJAN SAUCE)**

1 Mix all the marinade ingredients together with the steak and let stand for a minimum of 1 hour or as long as 3 to 4 hours.

2 Broil the steaks for about 2 minutes on each side. Or, should you wish, panfry the steaks in 1 tablespoon corn oil over moderate heat for 2 or 3 minutes.

3 Take 1 lettuce leaf, slather on it as much of the *samjan* hot sauce as wanted, add 1 or more *sookgat* leaves and a slice of steak. Wrap and eat.

Serve warm.

Serves 4.

Bangja Gui

BARBECUED BEEF IN A LETTUCE WRAPPER

Large lettuce leaves are a useful wrapper for steak with all the seasonings. Soft, flexible leaves such as Boston lettuce or the red or green crinkly varieties lend themselves to being folded into a round tube enclosing the steak. Everyone enjoys this style of sandwich as an appetizer with drinks.

1¼ ...... POUNDS SIRLOIN OR RIB STEAK

½ .... TEASPOON SALT

1 .... TABLESPOON PLUS 2 TEASPOONS SESAME OIL

¼ .... TEASPOON BLACK PEPPER

4 .... SCALLIONS, WHITE PART ONLY, CUT INTO JULIENNE STRIPS 2 INCHES LONG

3 .... TABLESPOONS SOY SAUCE

1 TO 3 ..... TEASPOONS HOT RED CHILI POWDER, TO TASTE

1 .... TEASPOON SUGAR

1 .... TABLESPOON TOASTED SESAME SEEDS

10 TO 12 .... LARGE LETTUCE LEAVES, WELL RINSED AND DRAINED

3 .... GARLIC CLOVES, SLICED THIN (OPTIONAL BUT RECOMMENDED)

1 Cut the steak into thin slices 3 inches long and 2 inches wide. This can be done easily if the steak is half frozen. Mix the steak with salt, 1 tablespoon sesame oil and the pepper; rub seasonings into the meat. Set aside for 15 minutes.

2 Soak the scallion slices in ice water for 15 minutes. Drain well. Mix together the soy sauce and the remaining 2 teaspoons sesame oil and toss this with the scallion slices. Set aside.

3 Mix the chili powder, sugar and sesame seeds together. Rub this seasoning, on the inside curl of the lettuce leaves. Set aside.

4 Grill the steak for 1 to 3 minutes for rare, medium or well done, according to taste, over charcoal or in a gas or electric broiler. Take 1 lettuce leaf, put several slices of steak in the center, add about 1 tablespoon of the seasoned scallions, a sliver or two of garlic, fold the lettuce over the steak and eat. Make as many sandwiches as you can eat.

Serve with rice and side dishes or as a glorified appetizer with drinks.

Serves 6.

Yuk Sanjook

The name for beef is *yuk* and *sanjook* is a skewer—a simple title for a collection of complex flavors in the Korean manner. This time it is black pepper that provides considerable verve rather than the hot chili. The beef and scallions on the skewers are assembled and pan-fried, which makes this an easy recipe to prepare in the American kitchen. You will need about 20 skewers.

1 ½ ..... **POUNDS BEEFSTEAK, ROUND OR SIRLOIN, CUT INTO SLICES 3 ½ INCHES LONG, ½ INCH WIDE AND ¼ INCH THICK**

1 ...... **TABLESPOON SUGAR**

5 ...... **TABLESPOONS SOY SAUCE**

2 ...... **TABLESPOONS TOASTED SESAME SEEDS**

1 ...... **TABLESPOON CHOPPED GARLIC**

4 ...... **TABLESPOONS CHOPPED SCALLION, GREEN PART ONLY**

2 ...... **TABLESPOONS KOREAN SESAME OIL**

½ ...... **TEASPOON BLACK PEPPER**

20 ..... **SCALLIONS (ABOUT), THE WHITE PART AND VERY FIRM GREEN CUT INTO 3-INCH LENGTHS**

1 Mix the beef and sugar together and let stand for ½ hour.

2 Now mix the soy sauce, sesame seeds, garlic, chopped scallion, 1 tablespoon of the sesame oil and the pepper together. Stir this into the beef.

3 Prepare the skewers. Alternate 5 pieces each of beef and scallion (white and firm green parts) on a skewer. Put the other tablespoon of sesame oil in a large skillet, add the skewers a few at a time, and fry over low heat for about 10 minutes.

Serve warm with rice, salads or your favorite combination of Korean side dishes.

Serves 6 to 8.

Nutari Beuseus Gochengi Bulgogi

BEEF AND MUSHROOM BARBECUE ON A SKEWER

Nutari is a type of edible agaric, a fungus or mushroom that has tentacles like an octopus but, of course, much smaller. These wild agarics are traditionally used in this barbecue but I have not seen them fresh in New York. If you can't find them, use the large-size supermarket mushrooms, which are to be sliced into halves lengthwise, through the stem. Soak 8 wood skewers in water for 1 hour to prevent burning.

- 3 ...... TABLESPOONS SOY SAUCE
- 2 ...... TABLESPOONS CHOPPED SCALLION
- 1 ...... TABLESPOON CHOPPED GARLIC
- 1 ...... TEASPOON KOREAN SESAME OIL
- 1 ...... TEASPOON TOASTED SESAME SEEDS, CRACKED
- ¼ ..... TEASPOON BLACK PEPPER
- 2 ...... TABLESPOONS SUGAR
- 12 ..... SCALLIONS, GREEN PART ONLY, CUT INTO 3-INCH-LONG PIECES
- ½ ..... POUND SIRLOIN OR FLANK STEAK, CUT INTO STRIPS ½ INCH WIDE, 3 INCHES LONG, ¼ INCH THICK
- ¼ ..... POUND MUSHROOMS, HALVED LENGTHWISE

1 Mix soy sauce, chopped scallions, garlic, sesame oil and seeds, pepper and sugar together well to make seasoning mix. Set aside.

2 Put 2 or 3 pieces of scallion on a skewer in a crosswise arrangement of slices, then the steak, then a mushroom and repeat 4 times to cover the skewer. Scallion, steak, mushroom in that order. Soak each skewer in the seasoning for ½ hour, turning it over once during this process.

3 The skewers may be cooked over charcoal (which is preferable), but a gas or electric grill may be used. Cook for about 5 minutes to be sure the meat is done.

Serve warm with rice, kimchi and your other favorite Korean side dishes.

Makes about 8 skewers.

Saegogi Gass

TENDER BEEF CUTLET

Several names are affixed to this cutlet. The modern Korean name is
noted above yet it is sometimes called "Beef Gass," mixing languages.
The ancient name for this is Chinese in origin—or *ooyook*, which
means "beef cutlet." The cutlet, without exotic seasoning and preparation, can be integrated into the American kitchen with ease.

½ ..... **TEASPOON SALT**

¼ ..... **TEASPOON PEPPER**

1 ...... **POUND SIRLOIN STEAK, CUT
INTO 4 PIECES ½ INCH THICK,
TRIMMED OF FAT**

2 ...... **GARLIC CLOVES, CRUSHED**

FLOUR FOR DREDGING

1 ...... **EGG, BEATEN WITH A FEW
GRAINS OF SALT**

DRIED BREAD CRUMBS

CORN OIL FOR PANFRYING

1 Sprinkle the salt and pepper on one side of each piece of steak
and rub in the crushed garlic. Let stand for 15 minutes.
2 Dredge each piece of steak with flour, dip into beaten egg, and roll
in the bread crumbs. Heat the oil in a skillet over moderate heat and
add the cutlets. Fry for 1 minute, then reduce heat to low and fry for
4 minutes on each side. This will be sufficient to brown the cutlets.
Remove and drain briefly on paper towels.

Serve warm with rice, salads and kimchi, and hot sauce should you
prefer more seasoning.

Serves 4 with other dishes.

Kalbi Jchim

BRAISED SHORT RIBS WITH CHESTNUTS AND MUSHROOMS

This braised beef is a delicious blend of the rich meat and the mellow taste of mushrooms and chestnuts—no chili powder.

The word *jchim* is a good example of the snag I ran into trying to spell Korean words phonetically. It is not pronounced jim or chim but an elision of the two.

1	MEDIUM-SIZE ONION
1	LARGE GARLIC CLOVE
5	SCALLIONS
1	HARD PEAR, PEELED AND CORED (OPTIONAL)
3	LARGE DRIED MUSHROOMS, SOAKED FOR 2 HOURS
2	TEASPOONS CORN OIL
1 ½	POUNDS SHORT RIBS OF BEEF WITH BONE, WELL TRIMMED OF FAT
2	TABLESPOONS SUGAR
1	TEASPOON KOREAN SESAME OIL
3	CUPS WATER
4	TABLESPOONS SOY SAUCE
2	MEDIUM-SIZE CARROTS, CUT INTO 1-INCH DIAGONAL PIECES
¼	POUND KOREAN RADISH, PEELED, CUT INTO 1-INCH CUBES
10	CHESTNUTS, PEELED, BOTH THE HARD SHELL AND THE INSIDE SKIN REMOVED
1	TEASPOON SESAME SALT
½	TEASPOON PEPPER

1 Chop the onion, garlic, scallions, and pear if used, into very small pieces. Set aside.
2 Drain the mushrooms, remove and discard the stems, and cut the caps into quarters. Squeeze lightly to remove excess water. Stir-fry in corn oil over moderate heat for 2 minutes. Set aside.
3 Put the ribs into a bowl with the sugar and knead for 1 minute. Add the sesame oil and knead the meat for another minute. Let stand for 10 minutes. Put the beef into a pan with the onion mixture, 3 cups water, 2 tablespoons of the soy sauce, the carrots and radish and bring to a boil. Cover the pan and cook over moderate heat for 1 hour.

4 Now add the mushrooms, chestnuts, sesame salt, pepper and the balance of the soy sauce. Cover the pan and cook over low heat for ¹/₂ hour. The sauce will reduce to a thick mélange, but should the liquid evaporate too quickly during this time, add another ¹/₂ cup water and continue cooking for the required time. There will be some sauce remaining.

Serve warm with rice and salads.

Serves 4.

VARIATION: *If fresh chestnuts are not available, use the dried, peeled ones. Soak in water for 2 hours, drain, and use as directed in this recipe.*

If no type of chestnut is available, then substitute ¹/₃ cup of pine nuts or ¹/₂ cup of canned gingko nuts. Add either one as directed in sequence.

Saegogi *Pyogo Basut Boekum*

STIR-FRIED STEAK AND DRIED MUSHROOMS

Korean dried mushrooms are quite marvelous. Walking through any public market in the cities one can see large burlap bags filled with mushrooms divided as to size and general quality. I purchased some in the city of Chonju that were from 3 to 4 inches in diameter. When reconstituted in water for an hour they expanded like thick, round steaks.

CORN OIL FOR FRYING
½ ...... **POUND FLANK OR SIRLOIN STEAK, CUT INTO THIN STRIPS**
4 ...... **LARGE DRIED MUSHROOMS (ABOUT 2 OUNCES), SOAKED IN WATER FOR 1 HOUR, DRAINED, CUT INTO STRIPS TO MATCH THE STEAK**
1 ...... **GARLIC CLOVE, CRUSHED**
½ ...... **TEASPOON SALT, OR TO TASTE**
2 ...... **SCALLIONS, CUT INTO 3-INCH PIECES**
1 ...... **TABLESPOON SOY SAUCE**
1 ...... **TEASPOON TOASTED SESAME SEEDS**
1 ...... **TEASPOON KOREAN SESAME OIL**

1 Heat the corn oil in a skillet or wok. Add the steak and stir-fry over moderate heat until it changes color, then add the mushrooms and garlic. Stir-fry for 2 minutes.

2 Now add the salt, scallions, soy sauce and sesame seeds and continue to fry for 2 minutes to integrate the flavors. At the last moment stir in the sesame oil.

Serve warm with white rice and side dishes of your choice.

Serves 4.

Songyee Basut Boekum

BEEF AND MUSHROOM STIR-FRY

Tender slivers of beefsteak of your choice furnish a rich meat flavor with a plethora of the white mushrooms. It is not necessary to include large quantities of meat since that is not the Korean way. Beef is expensive! The emphasis is on the mushrooms and simple seasonings.

- ¼......**POUND SIRLOIN OR FLANK STEAK, SLICED THIN**
- ½......**BEATEN EGG**
- 2 ......**TEASPOONS CORNSTARCH**
- 3 ......**TABLESPOONS CORN OIL**
- 2 ......**GARLIC CLOVES, CHOPPED FINE**
- 1 ......**TEASPOON SALT, OR TO TASTE**
- 10 .....**OUNCES FRESH WHITE MUSHROOMS, WELL RINSED AND HALVED LENGTHWISE THROUGH THE STEM**
- ½......**TEASPOON SUGAR**
- 2 ......**SCALLIONS, CUT INTO 3-INCH LENGTHS**
- ¼......**TEASPOON PEPPER**
- ½......**SEMI-HOT RED CHILI, SEEDED, SLICED THIN (¼ CUP)**

1 Mix the beef, egg and cornstarch together and set aside. This procedure is thought to tenderize the meat when it is too firm.
2 Heat the oil in a wok or large skillet. Add the beef and stir-fry for 1 minute over moderate heat. Add the garlic, salt and mushrooms and continue to stir-fry for 2 minutes.
3 Now add the sugar, scallions, black pepper and the red chili, which provides some color. Stir-fry for 2 minutes more. Adjust the salt if you wish at this time. Some liquid will accumulate with a very light thickening provided by the cornstarch.

Serve warm with rice, kimchi and salad.

Serves 4.

Kan Jun

This veal liver cutlet is simply prepared and popular in Korea. Koreans like all of the beef innards—the heart, tongue, kidneys and the liver—whether lightly fried as in this case, steamed plain or eaten raw and seasoned with sesame seeds and oil. The liver cutlet is a welcome contrast from traditional highly seasoned foods.

½ ..... POUND VEAL LIVER, WITH THE SKIN REMOVED

A FEW GRAINS OF SALT AND PEPPER

FLOUR FOR DREDGING

1 ...... EGG, BEATEN

2 ...... TABLESPOONS CORN OIL FOR PANFRYING

1 Soak the liver in cold water for 10 minutes to remove the blood. Drain and dry. Slice thin into 8 squares or rectangles. Sprinkle the pieces on each side with a few grains of salt and pepper. Score each piece twice with a sharp knife but not deeply. This keeps the liver flat when frying and prevents its curling up.

2 Dredge the liver lightly with flour, then dip into the beaten egg. Heat the oil in a skillet and fry each piece over low heat for about 2 minutes, or just enough to cook the liver but still retain its inner moisture. Drain briefly on paper towels.

Serve warm with other dishes that could include seafood, rice, several salads and kimchi of your choice.

Serves 4.

Jeyuk Sun

PORK AND POTATO SAUTÉ

Pork is a popular meat in Korea for several reasons, the principal one being that it is cheaper than the prestigious beef. The recipe here is extended and enriched with potato slices which absorb the seasonings and become meatlike. The substantial garnish completes a fine family-style dish, which can be prepared in large quantities.

1 .... POUND BONELESS PORK LOIN
4 .... SCALLIONS, SLICED ¼ INCH THICK
1 TO 2 ..... TEASPOONS GOCHU JANG PASTE, TO TASTE
2 .... TEASPOONS RICE WINE
3 .... TEASPOONS SUGAR
¼ .... TEASPOON PEPPER
1 .... GARLIC CLOVE, CRUSHED
1 .... INCH OF FRESH GINGER, CRUSHED
1 .... TABLESPOON SOY SAUCE
1 .... TABLESPOON PLUS 1 TEASPOON CORN OIL
2 .... MEDIUM-SIZE POTATOES, PEELED, CUT INTO ¼-INCH-THICK SLICES
1 .... CUP WATER
1 .... EGG, BEATEN
1 .... SEMI-HOT GREEN CHILI, SEEDED, CUT INTO 3-INCH-LONG JULIENNE STRIPS
1 .... SMALL ONION, SLICED (⅓ CUP)
½ .... TEASPOON TOASTED SESAME SEEDS
½ .... TEASPOON KOREAN SESAME OIL
¼ .... TEASPOON SALT

1 Cut the pork into strips 3 inches long, ½ inch wide and ¼ inch thick. Mix the slices with scallions, gochu jang, rice wine, sugar, pepper, garlic, ginger and soy sauce. Set aside for 15 minutes.
2 Heat 1 tablespoon oil in a pan and in it fry the potatoes over moderate heat just long enough to color them, about 3 minutes. Add the water and bring to a boil.
3 Add the pork and marinade to the pan, cover, and cook over moderate/low heat for about ½ hour, enough to evaporate almost all the liquid. Set aside until ready to serve.

(Continued next page)

4 Heat the 1 teaspoon oil in a skillet, add the egg and prepare a thin omelet. Remove it from the skillet and cool. Cut into strips 3 inches long and 1/2 inch wide.

5 Add the chili, onion, sesame seeds, oil and the salt to the same skillet and stir-fry over moderate heat until the vegetables have softened, about 3 minutes.

6 Put the pork and potato mixture into a serving platter and add the vegetables around the perimeter of the dish. Scatter the egg strips over the top. Or, another method, depending upon the cook, put the vegetables over the pork and scatter the egg strips over all.

Serves 6.

NOTE: *Note that the color of the pork sauté is important and this is provided by the red gochu jang which is also chili-hot. To those with tender palates, it might be prudent to add only 1 teaspoon gochu jang and 2 teaspoons tomato ketchup for color. This is a modern but an effective method of having it both ways.*

Taegi Kalbi Gui

BROILED PORK SPARE RIBS

Koreans cut their pork ribs long, wide and meaty—unlike the thin bones cut Chinese-style. The ribs are served in this case with the indispensable kimchi, any one of the 200 varieties, which are reputed to cut the oils and richness of the meat and encourage digestion.

6 ...... PIECES OF SPARERIBS WITH BONE (1 ½ POUNDS), CUT 4 TO 5 INCHES LONG, 2 INCHES WIDE AND 1 INCH THICK (OR BLADE CUT PORK CHOPS)

1 ...... TABLESPOON SUGAR

2 ...... TABLESPOONS SOY SAUCE

1 ...... TABLESPOON GOCHU JANG PASTE

1 ...... TEASPOON GINGER JUICE (ABOUT 1 TABLESPOON FRESH GINGER SQUEEZED THROUGH A GARLIC PRESS)

1 ...... GARLIC CLOVE, CRUSHED

1 ...... TEASPOON SESAME SEEDS

1 ...... TEASPOON KOREAN SESAME OIL

1 ...... TABLESPOON TOMATO KETCHUP (OPTIONAL)

1 Rinse the pork in cold water and dry. Add the sugar and mix well. Add the soy sauce, gochu jang, ginger juice, garlic, sesame seeds and oil and mix well. If the ketchup is used, include it at this time. Mix the pork and marinade together and let stand for at least 2 hours before using but preferably and traditionally overnight.

2 Put the ribs and sauce in a roasting pan, cover and bake in a 450°F. oven for 40 minutes. Turn over once after 20 minutes. Or broil in a gas or electric oven for 20 minutes or until brown and crisp. Or use the ancient method—barbecue over charcoal for 20 minutes.

Serve warm with rice, kimchi and salads.

Serves 4.

Jae Yook Gui

SEASONED PORK BARBECUE

The cut of pork belly that has 3 layers—the outer skin, a thick layer of fat below that, then a strip of lean meat—is preferred for this barbecue. The Chinese are also fond of this particular cut of meat and chunks are available for sale at the Chinese butcher.

2	POUNDS (IN 1 PIECE) 3-LAYER PORK BELLY, SLICED INTO LONG THIN STRIPS LIKE BACON
1	TABLESPOON WHITE OR RICE WINE
1	TEASPOON SUGAR
1	MEDIUM-SIZE ONION, SLICED THIN (1/2 CUP)
3	GARLIC CLOVES, SLICED THIN
1	INCH OF FRESH GINGER, SLICED THIN
2	SCALLIONS, SLICED THIN
1	TABLESPOON HOT RED CHILI POWDER (GOCHU GARU)
1/2	TEASPOON TOASTED SESAME SEEDS, CRUSHED
1	SWEET RED PEPPER, HALVED, SEEDED, THEN CUT INTO 8 EQUAL PIECES
1	TABLESPOON KOREAN SESAME OIL
2	TABLESPOONS SOY SAUCE
1/2	TEASPOON WHITE PEPPER

1 Put the pork slices in a large mixing bowl. Add the wine and sugar and mix well. Add the onion, garlic, ginger, scallions, chili powder, sesame seeds, sweet pepper, sesame oil, soy sauce and white pepper. Mix everything together and let the mixture stand at room temperature for 1 hour.

2 Ideally, one should broil the pork slices over charcoal but in the absence of that, a gas or electric broiler will do. Barbecue for several minutes until either medium or well done.

Serve with rice and your favorite side dishes.

Serves 6.

Samgyupsal

A special cut of fresh pork is used in this recipe which gives it its name.
Fresh pork belly found in Chinese and Korean butcher shops has 3 visible layers; there is the outer skin, then a 2-inch layer of thick fat and attached to that from 2 to 3 inches of lean meat. Nevertheless, the Samgyupsal is assembled so that the flavorful meat is used and the fat and skin discarded. The meat is glorified with a pine nut spice paste and garnished with omelets, semi-hot chili, mushrooms and tree ears. You will need about 1 yard twine in making this recipe.

Pork

- 1 ½..... **POUNDS FATBACK OR FRESH PORK BELLY, CUT INTO 2 SLABS, EACH ABOUT 6 INCHES LONG, 2 INCHES WIDE AND 3 INCHES THICK**
- 2 ...... **INCHES OF FRESH GINGER, SLICED DIAGONALLY**
- 5 ...... **CUPS WATER**

Seasoning Paste

- 1 ...... **TABLESPOON PINE NUTS, GROUND FINE IN A PROCESSOR**
- 1 ...... **TEASPOON CRUSHED FRESH GINGER, WITH JUICE**
- 1 ...... **TEASPOON FINE-CHOPPED SALTED BABY SHRIMP AND LIQUID**

Garnishes

- 1 ...... **EGG, SEPARATED**
- 2 ...... **TEASPOONS CORN OIL**
- 1 ...... **LARGE DRIED MUSHROOM, SOAKED IN WATER FOR 1 HOUR, DRAINED, SLICED THIN, STEM DISCARDED**
- 1 ...... **TABLESPOON DRIED TREE EARS, SOAKED IN WATER FOR 1 HOUR, RINSED WELL TO REMOVE SAND, THEN SLICED THIN**
- 1 ...... **YOUNG KIRBY CUCUMBER, GREEN SKIN AND ABOUT ¼ INCH PULP SLICED OFF LENGTHWISE AND CUT INTO 2-INCH-LONG JULIENNE STRIPS (DO NOT USE REST OF PULP AND SEEDS)**
- 1 ...... **SEEDED SEMI-HOT GREEN CHILI, CUT INTO VERY THIN DIAGONAL 2-INCH SLICES**

(Continued next page)

1 To prepare the pork, rinse it in cold water and drain. Using about 14 inches of light twine, wind it firmly 3 times around each slab and tie. This is to ensure that the pork remains flat during the cooking.

2 Put the pork, ginger and water into a large pan, bring to a boil and cover. Cook over moderate heat for 1 hour which is enough to tenderize the meat. The ginger seasons the pork and neutralizes any meat aroma. Remove the meat; cool for 10 minutes. Discard the ginger and broth.

3 To prepare the seasoning paste, mash the pine nuts, ginger and salted shrimp together. Set aside. The paste has a lightly salted, ginger, nutlike flavor completely compatible with the pork.

4 To prepare the garnishes, lightly beat the white and yolk separately with a few grains of salt. Heat a nonstick skillet with 1 teaspoon of the oil and add the egg white, swirling it around. Fry over low heat for a few seconds, then turn it over carefully and fry for a few seconds more, enough to set the omelet. Remove and set aside. Do the same for the egg yolk. When the omelets are cool, cut into 3-inch lengths, $1/8$ inch wide.

5 Stir-fry the mushroom slices in the other 1 teaspoon oil over moderate heat for about $1/2$ minute. This will evaporate some liquid and add flavor. Do the same for tree ears. Set both aside separately.

6 To assemble, remove the string from the pork slabs. With a sharp knife, carefully cut through lengthwise separating the meat and fat layers, but leave the 3 layers in position. Then cut slices $1/4$ inch wide almost all the way through the slab but leaving it still held together.

7 Cover the top of the pork with the seasoning paste. Push the white and yellow omelet slices in between the meat slices, but not enough to conceal them; they should be visible. Do this for all of the meat. Add a few slices of mushroom, tree ears, cucumber and chili to the top and between the meat slices, all the time arranging alternate colors of white, yellow and green.

8 Steam the garnished and seasoned pork slab in a Chinese-style steamer over moderate heat for 5 minutes. The fat and skin layers are left in place but ultimately discarded.

Serve warm, each diner pulling off slices of meat and garnish.

Serve with rice, various kimchis and, if you wish, Sangchussam, the Lettuce Sandwich (see p. 75).

Serves 4.

Don Gass

BREADED PORK CUTLET

This cutlet is not a purely Korean preparation. It is Japanese by invention
and Korean by adoption. Like so many foods around the world, the
recipe was brought in by immigrants or colonial people and absorbed
into the mainstream of the cuisine. Pork is of lesser popularity than
beef in Korea, but this well-known cutlet is a great favorite.

1 ...... **POUND BONELESS PORK FILLET
(4 SLICES)**

2 ...... **GARLIC CLOVES, CRUSHED TO A PASTE**

1 ...... **INCH OF FRESH GINGER, CRUSHED
TO A PASTE**

1 ...... **TEASPOON SALT**

1/4 ...... **TEASPOON PEPPER**

1/4 ...... **CUP FLOUR**

1 ...... **EGG, BEATEN**

1/4 ...... **CUP DRY BREAD CRUMBS**

CORN OIL FOR PANFRYING

1 Score one side of each slice of pork three times about 1/8 inch deep.
Rub into the scored cuts about 1/4 teaspoon each garlic and ginger.
Let stand for 15 minutes to marinate.

2 Sprinkle each slice with a few pinches of salt and pepper. Dust the
slices of pork with the flour, then dip into the beaten egg and cover
with the bread crumbs. Heat the oil in a skillet over moderate heat.

3 Fry the cutlets for about 3 minutes on each side to brown well.
Pork needs to be cooked through. Plunge a chopstick into each slice
to test doneness. If the hole fills with a pink liquid then more frying is
necessary. If the hole is dry, then the cutlet is done. Drain briefly on
paper towels.

Serve with rice, several kinds of kimchi and Korean salads.

Serves 4.

Sokkori Jchim

OXTAIL STEW

Oxtail has fallen out of favor in the American kitchen since it involves long cooking and is not beautiful to look at. The meat, however, is rich and dense and the bone produces a gelatinous sauce filled with flavor. The Koreans assemble the stew simply, with few seasonings, relying on the natural flavor of the meat. They cook it until the meat is tender but has not fallen off the bone. The cook must be vigilant in this delicate balance so that the meat is still attached to the tail bones.

10	CUPS WATER
2	POUNDS OXTAIL, CUT BY THE BUTCHER INTO 2-INCH SECTIONS
1	TABLESPOON CHOPPED GARLIC
½	TEASPOON PEPPER
2	MEDIUM-SIZE ONIONS, SLICED THIN (1 CUP)
1	TEASPOON SALT, OR TO TASTE
1	TABLESPOON SOY SAUCE
1 OR 2	WHOLE DRIED HOT RED CHILIES, SEEDED
1	SMALL SCALLION, CHOPPED

1 Bring the water to a boil in a large pan with the oxtail. Skim off the foam that rises and cook over moderate heat, covered, for about 2 hours to soften the meat. Do not overcook since you want the meat still attached to the bones. Remove the oxtail and set aside. Cool the broth, then chill it in the refrigerator (preferably overnight) to congeal the fat. Remove and discard the fat. Reserve the broth, which has reduced by half.

2 Put the garlic into the broth, bring to a boil, and simmer over low heat for 15 minutes. Then add the pepper, onions (which provide light sweetening), salt, soy sauce, chilies and oxtail and continue to cook for 20 minutes, which should reduce the liquid to about 1 cup. Add the chopped scallion and remove the pan from the heat.

Serve warm with rice, kimchi and salads.

Serves 4 to 6.

NOTE: To use a Pressure Cooker: *In my opinion, pressure cookers should have a more important place in the kitchen. Tough beef, tongue, beef shank and oxtail can be cooked easily and quickly without altering the character of the dish being prepared as occurs with that abomination of the twentieth-century kitchen—the microwave.*

To prepare this fine Oxtail Stew, put 2 cups water (instead of 10) into the pressure cooker plus all the other ingredients. Cook for 40 minutes, just enough to tenderize the oxtail. Open the cooker and test the tail to see if it is tender. If still too firm, continue to cook without pressure until tender. Also, if too much liquid has accumulated, reduce it over moderate heat until about 1 cup of sauce remains. I have found my Swiss-made, well-designed cooker of enormous assistance to me in the kitchen.

Dak Jchim

CHICKEN STEW

I am not convinced that this is a stew although it is a literal translation from Korean. Perhaps we should call it braised. The chicken is firm-textured, not falling off the bones, yet thoroughly cooked. The small amount of sauce that remains is intensely flavored and has permeated the vegetables. Korea's famous dried mushrooms have become a meat-like adjunct to the chicken and have absorbed the sauce.

4 ...... **LARGE DRIED MUSHROOMS**
2 ...... **POUNDS CHICKEN PARTS, 8 PIECES (THIGHS, LEGS, BREAST), LOOSE SKIN AND FAT DISCARDED**
2 ...... **TEASPOONS CORN OIL**
1 ...... **INCH OF FRESH GINGER, CHOPPED VERY FINE**
4 ...... **GARLIC CLOVES, CHOPPED FINE**
2 ...... **MEDIUM-SIZE ONIONS, CHOPPED COARSE (1 CUP)**
1 ...... **CUP WATER**
¼ ..... **CUP SOY SAUCE**
½ ..... **TEASPOON SUGAR**
2 ...... **CARROTS, SLICED DIAGONALLY INTO 1-INCH PIECES (2 CUPS)**
2 ...... **MEDIUM-SIZE POTATOES, PEELED, CUT INTO 1-INCH CUBES**
4 ...... **SCALLIONS, CUT INTO 2-INCH LENGTHS**
1 ...... **TEASPOON KOREAN SESAME OIL**

1 Cover the mushrooms completely with water and let them soak for 2 hours. Drain, cut them into halves and discard the stems.

2 Put the chicken into a pan without oil and stir-fry over moderate heat for 2 minutes. Add the corn oil and ginger and fry for 1 minute. Add the garlic and onions and stir-fry for another minute, stirring all the while.

3 Add the water, soy sauce, sugar, carrots, potatoes, mushrooms and scallions, cover the pan and cook over low heat for 25 minutes. Stir now and then. At the last moment, when the chicken will have become tender, add the sesame oil and cook for 5 minutes more. There is little sauce remaining but everything is moist and tender.

Serve warm with sticky rice and 3 or 4 side dishes of your choice.

Serves 4.

Dak Bulgogi

Boneless breast of chicken, simply seasoned Korean-style, and then grilled, is tender, flavorful, easily prepared and at the same time traditional. The same method is used in preparing beef strips and most Korean restaurants feature this classic.

1	**WHOLE CHICKEN BREAST**
1	**SLICE OF FRESH GINGER, SQUEEZED THROUGH A PRESS**
2	**GARLIC CLOVES, CRUSHED**
¼	**TEASPOON PEPPER**
1	**TEASPOON SESAME SALT**
1	**TABLESPOON SOY SAUCE**
1	**SCALLION, SLICED THIN**

1 Divide the chicken breast into 4 equal pieces. The 2 thick ends are to be cut almost through and folded open (butterflied). Mix the chicken and all the other ingredients together, rubbing the seasonings into the meat with your fingers. Marinate for at least 1 hour.

2 Grill over charcoal or in a gas or electric broiler for about 3 minutes, or long enough to cook the chicken through without drying it out. Turn the pieces over once during this time.

Serve warm with rice, salads and side dishes of your choice.

Serves 4.

Young Gye Beck Sook

STUFFED BABY CHICKEN IN BROTH

The title does not begin to reveal the various flavors that provide the
taste sensations in this Korean production. True exotics such as
Korean dates, the mystical ginseng, chestnuts, garlic (a lot of it) and
fresh ginger provide the broth and chicken with a unique richness,
texture and color. The Young Gye is considered to be a "white" dish
since nothing that would discolor the broth—neither soy sauce nor
scallions—is used.

During the hot summer days when it is not desirable to cook red
meat since it induces lethargy, the Young Gye is served in homes and
restaurants that specialize in it. It is the quintessential summer fare
served frequently in individual *tukbaeges*, 1 baby chicken per person.
A very generous serving.

1 ...... **SMALL CHICKEN OR CORNISH GAME HEN (1½ POUNDS)**

⅓ ..... **CUP SWEET (GLUTINOUS) RICE, WELL-RINSED IN COLD WATER**

10 ..... **GARLIC CLOVES, PEELED**

2 ...... **PIECES OF GINSENG, EACH 2 INCHES LONG (OPTIONAL BUT RECOMMENDED)**

½ ..... **INCH OF FRESH GINGER, SLICED**

5 ...... **DRIED KOREAN DATES**

5 ...... **PEELED CHESTNUTS**

1 ...... **TEASPOON SALT, OR TO TASTE**

2 ...... **SCALLIONS, SLICED THIN, FOR GARNISH**

1 Rinse out well the body cavity of the chicken with cold water.
Sew up the neck part to seal in the ingredients. Stuff the chicken
with the rice, 5 of the garlic cloves and ginseng if used. Sew up the
opening tightly.
2 Put the chicken in a large pan and add water just to the top of
the chicken. Add the ginger, the other 5 garlic cloves, the dates,
chestnuts and salt and bring to a boil over moderate heat. Skim off
and discard foam, reduce heat to low, cover the pan, and simmer
for 1 hour. About halfway through the time, turn the chicken over
to cook on the other side.

Serve warm in a large tureen. Break the chicken into 4 pieces and
serve each diner first the meat and stuffing and later the broth.

(Continued next page)

The garnish of scallion slices is to taste, each diner sprinkling as much as wanted in the broth.

Salt and pepper should be made available for those wishing a more intense flavor to the broth. Put 1 tablespoon coarse salt in a small dish with 1 teaspoon of black pepper in the center of the salt. Besides the stuffing, a dish of rice is served with the Young Gye. In this case, $1/2$ cup standard sticky rice and $1/2$ cup glutinous rice are cooked together, providing a different texture.

Serves 2.

Samgyetang

BABY CHICKEN AND GINSENG SOUP

This Samgyetang is a celebrated soup from the island of Cheju, and deservedly so since the prestigious, almost mystical, ginseng root is cooked and eaten like a vegetable with the chicken. The Samgyetang is cooked in a *tukbaege* and brought still bubbling to the table. It is considered to be a summer dish in restaurants and homes.

Koreans will break up the chicken and rice in the pot so that it becomes a gruel. I prefer that each person helps himself out of the pot, taking something of all the ingredients and spooning the rich, thick broth over all. It seems to me more aesthetic without altering the taste. The jujubes provide a touch of contrasting sweetness to the chicken, rice and ginseng.

Ginseng, or *insam* as it is also called in Korea, tastes to me like a slightly bitter parsnip. Its properties are alleged to be strengthening and bring about rejuvenation.

½ .... **CUP GLUTINOUS RICE, WELL-RINSED, OR ENOUGH TO FILL THE CHICKEN CAVITY LOOSELY**

2 .... **PIECES OF FRESH GINSENG ROOT, EACH 2 INCHES LONG**

1 .... **SCALLION, SLICED THIN**

6 .... **JUJUBES (KOREAN DATES)**

2 .... **GARLIC CLOVES, HALVED LENGTHWISE**

1 .... **SMALL CHICKEN OR CORNISH GAME HEN (ABOUT 1 POUND)**

2 .... **CUPS WATER**

1 .... **TEASPOON TOASTED SESAME SEEDS**

1 .... **TEASPOON KOREAN SESAME OIL**

⅛ .... **TEASPOON PEPPER**

1 Mix the rice, ginseng root, scallion, 3 of the jujubes and 1 garlic clove together and stuff the chicken. Sew up the opening.

2 Put the chicken in the *tukbaege* or in a heavy pot with a cover that is just a bit larger than the chicken. Add the 2 cups water, the other 3 jujubes, the other garlic clove, the sesame seeds and sesame oil and the pepper. Bring to a boil, cover the pot and reduce heat to low. Simmer over low heat for 1 hour.

The soup will develop a thick, cloudy consistency and the chicken will soften enough to melt away from the bones.

Serve hot in the *tukbaege* if you have one, or transfer the chicken and broth to a large serving bowl.

Serves 2 with a variety of side dishes.

Dak Gochu Jang Boekum

CHICKEN IN A HOT CHILI SAUCE

Koreans in the southern part of the country like salty and chili-hot foods. The cities of Kwangju and Chongju in southwest Korea, where I spent some culinary research time, are centers for this hot salty dish.

- 2 ...... **POUNDS CHICKEN PARTS (BREAST, THIGH, WINGS), LOOSE SKIN AND FAT DISCARDED**
- 5 ...... **TABLESPOONS SUGAR**
- 1 ...... **TABLESPOON CHOPPED GARLIC**
- 1 ...... **SCALLION, CHOPPED**
- 1 ...... **TABLESPOON CHOPPED FRESH GINGER**
- 2 ...... **TABLESPOONS SOY SAUCE**
- 5 ...... **TABLESPOONS GOCHU JANG**
- 2 ...... **TABLESPOONS KOREAN SESAME OIL**
- 2 ...... **TABLESPOONS TOASTED SESAME SEEDS**
- 1/2 ...... **CUP WATER**

1 Cut the chicken into 3-inch pieces. Divide the wings. Mix the parts with the sugar and marinate for 1 hour or more. (The sugar is a tenderizer.)
2 Mix together all the other seasonings—garlic, scallion, ginger, soy sauce, gochu jang, sesame oil and sesame seeds. Mix well, add to the chicken, and marinate for another hour.
3 Pour the 1/2 cup of water into a pan and bring to a boil. Add the chicken and marinade and simmer, covered, over low heat for about 1/2 hour, which is enough to cook the chicken and evaporate nearly all the liquid. Stir the mixture once or twice during this process.

Serve warm with rice, salads and kimchi.

Serves 6.

Dak Gan Kong Pat Cochigui

CHICKEN LIVER, HEART AND
VEGETABLES ON A SKEWER

Although these skewered meats may be cooked over charcoal or as in
modern times, over small gas table broilers, this barbecue is panfried
with the smallest amount of oil and for just a few minutes. A black
pepper, salt and sesame-oil dip provides a powerful mix that accents
the neutral foods on the skewers.

½ ..... POUND CHICKEN LIVERS
½ ..... POUND CHICKEN HEARTS
3 ...... TEASPOONS SALT
1 ...... TABLESPOON CHOPPED GINGER
4 ...... CUPS WATER
4 ...... SCALLIONS (WHITE PART ONLY),
CUT INTO 1 ½-INCH PIECES
1 ...... GREEN PEPPER, CUT INTO
1-INCH SQUARES
2 ...... TEASPOONS BLACK PEPPER
1 ...... TABLESPOON KOREAN SESAME OIL
¼ ..... CUP CORN OIL

1 Put the chicken livers, hearts, 1 teaspoon of the salt, the ginger,
and 4 cups water into a pan. Bring to a boil and cook over moderate heat for 10 minutes. Drain well and cool. Cut the livers into
¾-inch pieces.
2 Put three pieces of liver and heart on each skewer and inter-
sperse with pieces of scallion and green pepper. Prepare all the
meats and vegetables this way.
3 Mix together the other 2 teaspoons salt, the black pepper and
sesame oil into a paste to make a seasoning as well as a dip when
the meat is served. Dab each piece of meat and vegetable with the
seasoning paste. Heat the corn oil in a skillet and fry the skewers, a
few at a time, over moderate heat for ½ minute on each side. Dab
more of the seasoning on if you wish to have a more assertive flavor.

Serve warm with rice, salads or any other Korean foods.

Serves 4.

Index

Table of Equivalents

The exact equivalents in the following tables have been rounded for convenience.

US/UK

oz = ounce
lb = pound
in = inch
ft = foot
tbl = tablespoon
fl oz = fluid ounce
qt = quart

METRIC

g = gram
kg = kilogram
mm = millimeter
cm = centimeter
ml = milliliter
l = liter

WEIGHTS

US/UK	Metric
1 oz	30 g
2 oz	60 g
3 oz	90 g
4 oz (¼ lb)	125 g
5 oz (⅓ lb)	155 g
6 oz	185 g
7 oz	220 g
8 oz (½ lb)	250 g
10 oz	315 g
12 oz (¾ lb)	375 g
14 oz	440 g
16 oz (1 lb)	500 g

OVEN TEMPERATURES

Fahrenheit	Celsius	Gas
250	120	½
275	140	1
300	150	2
325	160	3
350	180	4
375	190	5
400	200	6
425	220	7
450	230	8
475	240	9
500	260	10

LIQUIDS

US	Metric	UK
2 tbl	30 ml	1 fl oz
¼ cup	60 ml	2 fl oz
⅓ cup	80 ml	3 fl oz
½ cup	125 ml	4 fl oz
⅔ cup	160 ml	5 fl oz
¾ cup	180 ml	6 fl oz
1 cup	250 ml	8 fl oz
1½ cups	375 ml	12 fl oz
2 cups	500 ml	16 fl oz
4 cups/1 qt	1 l	32 fl oz

LENGTH MEASURES

⅛ in	3 mm
¼ in	6 mm
½ in	12 mm
1 in	2.5 cm
2 in	5 cm
3 in	7.5 cm
4 in	10 cm
5 in	13 cm
6 in	15 cm
7 in	18 cm
8 in	20 cm
9 in	23 cm
10 in	25 cm
11 in	28 cm
12/1 ft	30 cm

Bibliography

Cornell University. *Hortus Third Dictionary of Plants*. New York: The Macmillan Company, 1976.

Everett, Thomas H. *The New Botanical Garden Illustrated Encyclopedia of Horticulture*, vol. 7. New York and London: Garland Publishing Co., Inc., 1981.

Farrell, Kenneth T. *Spices, Condiments, and Seasonings*. AVI Book. New York: Van Nostrand Reinhold, 1990.

Ki-Baik Lee. *A New History of Korea*. Cambridge, MA: Harvard University Press, 1984.

Lee Wade's Korean Cookery. Seoul, Korea: Hollym International Corp., 1987.

Oriental Herbs and Vegetables. Brooklyn Botanic Garden Record, vol. 39. Brooklyn: Brooklyn Botanic Garden, 1983.

The Oxford Book of Food Plants. London: Oxford University Press, 1975.

Rosengarten, Frederick, Jr. *The Book of Spices*. New York: Jove Publications, 1981.